S. P. Marsh

from his friend

Y. B. Coddington

New York March 21. 1881

SERMONS

OF THE CITY

BY

HENRY C. POTTER, D.D.

Author of "Sisterhoods and Deaconesses at Home and Abroad,"
"The Gates of the East," etc.

NEW YORK
E. P. DUTTON & COMPANY
1881

Press of
J. J. Little & Co.,
10 Astor Place, N. Y.

St. Johnland
Stereotype Foundry,
Suffolk Co., N. Y.

TO

THE MEN AND WOMEN

OF

GRACE CHURCH, NEW YORK,

TO WHOM

THESE SERMONS WERE PREACHED

AND

TO WHOSE HELP AND SYMPATHY I OWE SO MUCH,

𝔗𝔥𝔦𝔰 𝔙𝔬𝔩𝔲𝔪𝔢 𝔦𝔰 𝔍𝔫𝔰𝔠𝔯𝔦𝔟𝔢𝔡.

INTRODUCTORY NOTE.

——o——

In complying with the request of my friend, its publisher, for this volume, I have reserved to myself the privilege of confining it mainly to such sermons as discuss those social problems imperfectly suggested by its title.

I need hardly say that this is not because I underestimate the importance of those other themes with which it is the province of the pulpit chiefly to deal, but because the questions considered in the following pages are among the most urgent of those that at present challenge attention. A living Church must needs have something to say to such questions, and unless at least their gravity and importance are candidly recognized, it can not expect to retain its hold upon thoughtful people. I am not so presumptuous as to suppose that the following pages offer a complete solution of the problems which they discuss, but I shall be glad if any word of mine shall lead others to attempt such a solution or to consider those problems for themselves.

H. C. P.

Grace Church Rectory,
  Advent: 1880.

CONTENTS.

SERMON XX.

COST AND BEAUTY IN CHRISTIAN WORSHIP.

SERMON XXI.

FAITH AND CULTURE.

SERMON XXII.

THE ULTIMATE TEMPLE.

SERMONS OF THE CITY.

SERMON I.

ST. PAUL IN THE MARKET-PLACE.

ACTS XVII. 16, 17.

"Now while Paul waited for them at Athens, his spirit was stirred within him, when he saw the city wholly given to idolatry. Therefore disputed he in the synagogue with the Jews, and with the devout persons, and in the market daily with them that met with him." *

THE thing that first strikes us here is that St. Paul seems to have had so little thought of his own dignity. We find him, while at Athens, in the synagogue on the Sabbath, and among the proselytes, or devout persons,—the converts to the Jewish faith,—as at other times; but he did not stay among them, and, as we find out by reading on a little farther, his most efficient work was accomplished when he turned his back upon the synagogue and the proselytes, and went down, daily, into the market-place.

The market-place of Athens was at once its exchange, its lyceum, and its lounge. Here assembled not only the traffickers in that commerce which reached from the Piræus to the distant coast of

---

* New York, March 11th, 1877.

Africa, but the agents and representatives of that other commerce which consists in the exchange not of commodities but of ideas. Men of all ranks and classes, of all callings and professions met and jostled each other in that eager throng, of which, four hundred years before, Demosthenes had said that it was more curious to hear the news and to listen to the last excitement than to recognize the impending destruction which threatened the liberties of the people. Here the loiterers sauntered among the plane-trees of the agora, here the philosophers gathered in knots beneath the porticos, and hither too, turned, day after day, the feet of that undaunted missionary whose words, ere he was done, were destined to shake the fabric of Athenian society to its very foundations.

Yes, hither, rather than to the court, the palace, or the Areopagus. The Athens of St. Paul's day, though very different from the Athens of earlier and mightier days had still its executive, its governors and its judges. Over that gay and restless people here presided an authority which was clothed with the most august sanctions and vested in its most venerable citizens. But the apostle has nothing to say to these, and does not seem to have sought them out at all. He answers, indeed, when later he is arraigned before the judge of the Areopagus, as he was in duty bound; but the chosen field of his efforts is not the precincts of the court, but the meet-

ing-place and the conscience of the common people.
He did not wait for the people to come to him—he
went to them; and those to whom he went were not
the rulers, the leaders, the authorities of the hour;
but rather those whose only influence was the influence of personal character, and whose best service to
the cause which the apostle had at heart,—if ever
they should be induced to render that service,—must
needs be the service of individual example.

Have you ever noticed that, in the history of that
new religion of which the apostle was the messenger,
it was always so? The Scribes and Pharisees of John
the Baptist's day sought him out, but he never sought
or courted them. Herod sent for John and for a season heard him gladly, but John never hung about the
court of Herod, and on those rare occasions when he
was summoned to the royal presence, uttered most
unpleasant truths, and uttered them with great plainness. Nay, Christ Himself, when He comes, discloses
all the way through a singular and almost surprising
indifference to the reformation of either the religious
or secular rulers of the time. One can not help thinking how different it might have been if Pontius Pilate
had been won to be the friend of the infant faith,
instead of being left to be the tool of its enemies.
And, when we follow the history of St. Paul, we are
reminded again and again, of opportunities when men
who were at least curious about the new doctrine

might, as it almost seems to us, have easily been won to exchange their curiosity for discipleship. Agrippa sends for the apostle, Felix sends for him, and so does Festus. There was no want of opportunity to make an impression in high places—and yet, the new religion resolutely sought the low ones.

It has been commonly supposed that this was because the new religion aimed to testify to its sympathy with the masses. It was not meant for the few, but for the many. It was not aristocratic, it was democratic. Its Founder was not one of the "privileged classes," He was a mechanic. Its message was not to self-complacency, but to conscious sorrow and want and need. And so it turned away from courts and palaces and royalty, and went where sorrow and want and need were most surely to be found.

All of which is true enough, but by no means the whole truth. The new religion turned its footsteps to the market-place, because, with a divine intuition, it discerned that in the renewal and ennoblement and transformation of the passions and ambitions, the hopes and interests of the market-place was to be found the redemption of humanity. Plato had said long before, that "no relief would ever reach the ills of men until either statesmen became philosophers, or philosophers assumed the government of states." To him, in other words, the only hope of the commonwealth was in a perfect system of government, perfectly administered. "Let us have," said the Greek mind in its attempt to solve the social problem, "let us have wise and blameless rulers, administering just and equal laws. Let us eliminate corruption and favoritism from the centres of power, and then you will have a free, prosperous, and virtuous people. Let us have a noble theatre, nobly administered, and then the part which the individual shall play will be as noble as are his surroundings. A wise and righteous management, grand scenery and a generous opportunity will secure grand and noble acting."

It is what many of us are saying, or thinking, to-day. Recent events have kindled in many quarters a resurrection of hope in regard to our national future, which is certainly not more instructive than it is pathetic. The apparent tokens of a disposition on the part of those in authority, to administer the government upon broad and national rather than on narrow and partisan principles, has been greeted with an enthusiasm which shows how indestructible in the heart of a nation as of a man, is hope, and how scanty are the foundations on which that hope is forever ready to rear its castles in the air. I am no pessimist nor dismal prophet of evil, and no man who respects himself or his neighbor, will be willing too hastily to distrust those tokens of honest and equit-

able and high-minded purpose which have lately come
to us from those who are now in high places. May
God give them wisdom and faith and courage for the
large and onerous and thankless task that is before
them, and may no brave and generous promise of
reform sink down into the traditional ruts of a narrow and partisan performance !

But, meantime, the truth for us to remember at
all times, and especially in these times, is the truth
that the hope of a nation is not in its forms of government, nor in the wisdom and equity of its executive,
nor in the justice and purity of its administration, so
much as in the elevation and redemption of individual
character among its people. Is it said that we must
take men as we find them ?—is it urged, in what has
expressively been described as the maxim of a prudent
despair, that you must adjust the machinery of government and the ordering of life to the inevitable
weaknesses and sins of men ?—is it urged again, that,
in the vast problem of bettering the world the only
immutable factor is man, and that he must be let
alone, save as he can be made to produce a new
result by being worked into new conditions ? The
answer of the religion of the New Testament is that
without waiting to reconstruct governments, we must
begin by striving for the new-creation of individual
character,—that without seeking merely to initiate
reforms in the council chamber, we must begin by

proclaiming the mind and will of God to men in the market-place, and, speaking to that in them which, howsoever defaced or deteriorated is, all the while, His divine image,—that love of the truth, that sense of the right, that instinct of upward aspiration which is in no human soul quite stifled or extinguished,— must shake them, thus, out of the lethargy of sin, and arouse them, rather, into a new-born life of righteousness.

And, in just so far as it has won any substantial victories, it is thus that the religion of Christ has worked from the beginning. If it has triumphed any- where, or at all, it has triumphed because it has made its appeal to the individual soul, seeking out and speaking to that soul in the street, in the home, in the market-place, wherever it could find it—press- ing upon it an individual message—pointing to that incomparable Being who once breathed out His life upon a cross, as a personal Saviour, and asking that to Him the heart should give the tribute of a per- sonal faith and devotion.

Meantime, we can not overlook the fact that side by side with this appeal, there have gone forward the triumphs of an advancing civilization and a lof- tier culture. When the Church points to what the faith of the Crucified has done for the individual life, the apostles of learning and of science point with an equal, if not a greater, pride to what these

have done for society and the state. Once, say
they, letters were the property of the Church, and
science the sole possession of a priesthood. But see,
since the emancipation of learning from the thraldom of priest-craft, what strides have been made by
the great communities of Europe and our own land,
—what culture has been widened and cheapened,
what institutions of art and science have been reared,
what scholars have been bred and nurtured within
them, what invention has revolutionized the habits
of our daily life and conquered the most insurmount-
able obstacles.

And indeed, who of us can see this without an
equal impulse of wonder and admiration? But who
of us can see it without seeing also, something more,
that has invariably gone along with it? With the
growth of wealth there has come the growth of poverty; with the multiplication of the arts, the multiplication of evil uses to which those arts may be
turned; with the birth of new sciences, there has confronted us the birth of new and hateful vices. Who
of us is not awed into silence, as he sees, for the
first time, the splendors of a great capital like London or Paris or Vienna? What perfection of civic
administration; what wisdom and foresight in the
use of wealth to achieve stately and imposing results; what manifold conveniences for the benefit
and comfort of the people! And, within a stone's

throw of some tall palace or some stately museum of art, what festering courts and tenements; what wretchedness and misery, and moral and physical degradation; what unnamable vices; what dire want; what utter and shameless infamy! Is this, we ask, the product of the highest civilization, of the largest freedom, of "the best government that the sun ever shone upon," and if it is, how is it better than that barbarism on which, so complacently, it professes to look down?

To such questions as these there can be but one answer. There is not a reform in which you and I are interested which has not its place and function in the bettering of human society. There is not a science or an art which may not be the handmaid of a better and purer social life. Above all, there is not a single step in the purification of our forms of government, in the elevation of our standards of political service and administration, in the emancipation of our vast political machinery from all sordid or merely partisan uses, that is not a step in the right direction. But the millennium will never come by that road. You may make government as just, as uncorrupt, as inflexibly impartial as was Aristides. You may make the streams of official patronage and power as pure and as wholesome as the sparkling waters of a mountain spring. But you can not cure a cancer with spring water. You can not restore the lost reason by means of a wholesome diet and a padded cell. "There is a spirit in man," wrote one long ago, "and the inspiration of the Almighty giveth him understanding." To that spirit, separately, severally, personally, something must speak, and speak as with a message from God. And so we find the apostle as the messenger of that spirit, pleading and arguing in the market-place. How hopeless it must have seemed at first! With what a light laugh they must have listened to this "babbler," as some of them called him. How useless, his fellow Israelites kept assuring him, doubtless, was any attempt to get a hearing there! It is the same cry that we are hearing every day, here and now. What are you going to do about the ever-increasing mass of people in this great city who are growing up in as genuine heathenism as any that is to be found in Dahomey? How do you propose to deal with the closely packed ranks of foreigners and strangers who are crowded into our tall tenement houses and thronging our lengthening streets? How vain to attempt to gain an entrance or to make an impression there!

Thank God that the apostle was wiser, and knew better, than this. He knew that in the market-place then, as in the tenement now, there beat the same human hearts and ached the same unanswered wants that were throbbing anywhere else. He knew that

there was no one so degraded, so selfish, so hardened but that somewhere in him there was the small
crevice through which the truth could find its way.
Above all, he knew that the more hopeless was the
darkness the more urgent was the need and call for
light. And so he begins at the bottom,—in the
market-place,—with the individual soul. He takes
his message to men, and does not wait for men to
come to his message. In all that he says there is, it
is true, no lowering or qualifying or abating of the
truth to square it with their notions to whom he
spoke. On the contrary, how clear, how manly he
is as he stands there in the agora crying, "The times
of your ignorance God hath winked at, but now He
commandeth all men everywhere to repent!"

This message of the apostle, a personal message
to the personal soul, is mine to you to-day. I have no
other. This religion of ours, this house, these acts
of worship—what do they all mean? Is it a pastime
for Sundays, or is it a message and a mandate for Sundays and week-days alike? Will you hearken to it only
here, or will you own its authority in the house and
in the market-place as well? Is it an adjunct simply
of our modern civilization, or is it a personal message
to your personal souls? Believe me there are no
other questions in all the world so instant and so
urgent as these. If the world is to become better,
it must become better because we have consented

to become better. If vice is to slink away abashed,
before the reign of a purer and loftier and juster era
in politics and in society, it must be because that
era has been inaugurated, first of all, in your breast
and in mine. And so the question is, whether or
no we will begin the work of national, political,
social, personal reform right here.

In urging such reform upon you it is my business
to hold up before you here a high ideal, and to bid
you at whatever cost, to strive to realize it. Not
unfrequently, I am told, with a frankness for which
I am most surely not ungrateful, that these ideals
are so high that they are simply discouraging. "It
is all very well," it is said, "to draw these portraitures
of imaginary virtue. But who of us can pretend to
reach them ? What is the use of setting up an impossible mark of attainment only to daunt one by
the dismal discrepancy of his own endeavors." And
yet, who of us would be genuinely contented with
any other ? Our aims may not be high, our inter-
sts may not be spiritual, our affections may not be
aspiring. But is it not true that when, from those
loftier levels from which the Master speaks His truth,
that truth comes trembling down to our souls, there
is something in us that answers to it ? Would we
have the strain of that celestial message lowered and
weakened or adulterated ? Is it not true that, when
some one standing beside us—some friend or neighbor

or acquaintance—speaks to us a manly and tender word about that Lord who hath bought us with His own blood and who longs to flood our lives with His own quickening Spirit, there is something in us that owns and welcomes such a word ? Are all our interests so worldly and fleeting, are all our affections so engrossed and satisfied that we have no ear for the voice of infinite wisdom and the message of redeeming love ? We have all heard of those in whom reason, dethroned by grief or calamity, has been suddenly and completely restored. After all other means had been tried, and tried in vain, some one has played the strains of a familiar air, and the simple melody, stealing into the crevices of the darkened mind, has burst the bonds of its imprisonment and flooded it in an instant with light and hope and life.

Even so, I think, it must have been with more than one of those to whom the apostle spoke in that busy market-place at Athens. There were some, there—yes, some, at any rate—who were carrying heavy and unshared burdens upon their hearts, and, who, beneath the thin disguise of their mirth and gaiety, were hiding a sorrowful spirit. With what unspeakable thankfulness, when at last they heard of Him who had come to lift off the burden of their sins and fears, and to give to them the secret of a life which drew its strength from that enduring life which is hid with Christ in God,—with what un-

speakable thankfulness then must they have turned
to Him and gladly laid their heavy burden at His
feet !

And what they did the Master comes, to-day,
and bids us do. He comes to us just as we are,—
if not at this moment in the market-place, yet, too
often, with our thoughts and hopes fuller of the life
that now is, than of any other life, and longing more
for what the world can give us than for any thing
beyond it. And yet—because, along with this, there
is another and a deeper longing which we can not
wholly stifle, He bids us own that longing—He bids
us lay our burden at His feet, and so find rest and
peace.

SERMON II.

"HE BELD THE CITY."

ST. LUKE XIX. 41.

*" And when He was come near, He beheld the city, and wept over it." **

WHATEVER else may have been characteristic of the earthly ministry of Jesus, it was pre-eminently wanting in alternations of strong emotion. So far as we know, He never laughed, and on only two occasions is it recorded of Him that He wept. And this was an element of His power. The people who most deeply move others are not the people who are most easily moved themselves. A man who is subject to every gust of emotion is not the man who can most powerfully influence either the feelings or the judgments of others. On the contrary, it was the calm and unimpassioned equipoise of Christ that conquered the homage even of His enemies. I do not wonder that art has striven to paint for us the chastened majesty of those last hours when the Saviour of the world confronted the malice of the chief priests. But it has striven only to fail. There was

---

* New York, March 23d, 1879.

something grander than art could grasp or canvas
depict in the kingly reserve of Jesus. How serenely
He moved among men! How little He was elated
by what seemed to be success, or depressed by what
seemed to be failure! How no provocation ever hurried Him out of that calm and lofty composure!
And yet we are told, here, that "when He came
near and beheld the city, He wept over it."

It is this—the tears of such a Being—that affects us.
In his oration after the death of Webster, Mr. Choate
has preserved an incident which was probably, in the
history of that great statesman, without a parallel.
He was arguing the case of his *alma mater*, Dartmouth
College, before the supreme court of the United States
at Washington. He had ended his plea and was about
to take his seat. Standing for some moments in silence he turned to the chief justice and said, "This,
sir, is my case! . . . You may destroy this little
institution. I know it is one of the lesser lights in
the literary horizon of our country. You may put it
out. But if you do, you must carry through your
work. You must extinguish one after another all
those great lights of science which for more than a
century have thrown their radiance over our land!

"It is, sir, as I have said, a small college. And yet,
there are those who love it." At this point the feelings which he had thus far succeeded in controlling
broke forth. His lips quivered, his firm cheek trem-

bled with emotion, his voice choked, and he seemed struggling to the utmost simply to gain that mastery over himself which might save him from an unmanly burst of feeling. In a few broken words, impossible justly to report, he went on to speak of his attachment to the college. The whole seemed to be mingled with the recollection of father, mother, brother, and all the trials and privations through which he had made his way into life. Every one saw that it was wholly unpremeditated, a pressure on his heart which sought relief in words and tears.

Wrote one who saw it, "The court-room during these two or three minutes presented an extraordinary spectacle. Chief Justice Marshall with his tall, gaunt figure bent over to catch the slightest whisper; Mr. Justice Washington at his side with his small, emaciated frame and a countenance looking like marble, leaning forward with an eager, troubled look; and the remainder of the court at the two extremities all pressing as it were toward a single point. . . . . One thing it showed me, that pathos depends not merely on the words uttered, but still more on the estimate which we put on him who utters them. There was not one among the strong-minded men of that assemblage who could think it unmanly to weep, when he saw, standing before him, the man who had made such an argument melted into the tenderness of a child."

Such an incident helps us to understand that other which is told us in the words of the text. If Peter's vision had been quickened as he stood there, beside his Master, until he, too, saw what Christ saw as he looked down upon the thronged and busy city at his feet, his tears would neither have surprised nor affected us. Peter was a man of eager and impulsive feeling, and the fountain of his grief was a spring that lay very near the surface. But that Peter's Master, who so often rebuked the hasty emotions of His disciple,— that He should have wept, at once touches and impresses us profoundly.

I. Why did He weep? It has been supposed that the picture of that approaching ruin and desolation which was coming so rapidly upon the unconscious capital, at once appalled and overwhelmed Him. He sketches that picture in strong and rapid strokes Himself. "The days shall come upon thee, that thine enemies shall cast a trench about thee, and compass thee round, and keep thee in on every side, and shall lay thee even with the ground, and thy children within thee; and they shall not leave in thee one stone upon another." It was a dark and dismal picture. And that which added to it an element of profoundest gloom, was the unconsciousness of those whom such a doom was threatening. Scarce a soul in Jerusalem seems to have been greatly sensi-

ble either of the national decadence or of its own individual peril. The pride of the Jew, like the pride
of the Spaniard, seemed to be as haughty in defeat
as in triumph, and as insolent always as though there
were nothing to fear. And yet the sceptre of Israel
had departed. The king was a puppet and his throne
a jest. By any ear that listened, the tramp of Roman
legions threatening the city and the temple might
already be distinctly heard, though it was nearly forty
years later before the troops of Titus trampled priests
and women under the cruel hoofs of a relentless cav-
alry. And all that Christ saw, as He stood there
and looked down upon beautiful Jerusalem—as distinctly as though it were happening at that very
moment!

Must it not have been this that made Him weep?
I do not doubt that it was an element in that divine
and unmatched sorrow. But that sorrow loses its
profoundest significance unless we see that it had
another and deeper element still. What is it, that
in the thought of a wise and good man costs him the
deepest pang when he encounters the waywardness
and wrong-doing of his own child? Is it merely that,
as he looks forward, he sees the inevitable misery
which that waywardness will entail? Is he thinking
about the bitter penalty which no young life can ever
escape that snatches the helm of its destiny out of
some wiser guidance, and makes its own ignorance or

passion or self-will the pilot of its future? Yes, he must needs think of that, if he has lived long enough in the world to learn that you can no more disconnect sin from suffering than you can disconnect seed-time and harvest. But you may be sure that such a parent is thinking of something else with a keener anguish still. He is thinking, "What must the nature be that is so insensible to love and duty and goodness!" He is thinking, "What are the moral sensibilities of one to whom baseness and ingratitude and wrong-doing are such easy and instinctive things!" He is thinking, "What have I to hope for from a child whose ruling impulses come out in deeds like these!"

And even so, I think, it was with Christ. Nay, we are not left to our surmises. His own words tell us what made Him weep. "If thou hadst known," He cries, "even thou in this thy day the things which belong unto thy peace! But now they are hid from thine eyes!" It was this spectacle of human insensibility, of eyes that would not see, and of ears that would not hear, that broke the Saviour down. It was the consciousness that the temple and the sanctuary, Mount Zion and the Holy Place, were all alike girt about by a people that did not care. He had spoken to them and they had not hearkened. The Being who had led their fathers out of their bitter bondage into a goodly land, and who had in so many ways revealed Himself in love and mercy to them, had

come again in that era of national misfortune and
humiliation, and they had not been willing to listen
to Him. The love of goodness, the longing for righteousness, the aspiration for nobleness and spiritual
emancipation—these were dead in them. And it was
this that made Christ weep. He could pity their
coming sorrow, and He did. But His heart ached,
most of all, as He contemplated that inmost evil in
them which made those sorrows so necessary and so
inevitable.

What made Christ weep ought to make us weep,
no less. These words of His compel us to think of
the sins and the sorrows of a great city. Have you
ever thought of ours? Would you care to see and
know them? A public speaker lately suggested the
revelations which would startle us if, like Asmodeus
in the fable, we could lift off the roofs of the homes
of the poor, and look down on the misery which
they would disclose to us. God knows we should
doubtless see more than one spectacle that would
drive sleep from our eyes and complacency from our
breasts. For we should see want and ignorance and
brutality such as only the strong contrasts and peculiar perils of a crowded population in an era of
high civilization can produce. But if we would know
the uttermost miseries of a great city we should not
find them in the homes of the poor. The things that
would appall us most would not be the squalor and

brutishness and crime of Mulberry Street, for, given
Mulberry Street and the death-breeding barracks that
line it, and the intemperance and crime that reign
there are as indissolubly related as heat and rotten-
ness. But that which, in a great city, must needs
most oppress one is, that when you have made men's
homes bright and spacious and beautiful you have
not thereby necessarily redeemed or ennobled those
who live in them. Given the culture of Phidias and
the wit of Alcibiades, given the grace of Cleopatra
and the charms of Aspasia, and you have thereby
secured neither the love of goodness nor a reverence
for God. It is possible to be as wise as Solon, and as
mean as Seneca, and when rare gifts are united to a
profound moral insensibility, then the case becomes
equally appalling and pathetic.

But a great city is made up neither of rich people
nor of poor people. In our own community the great
majority are neither paupers nor merchant princes.
They are that vast middle class of artisans and
tradesmen, and men and women, of which all great
populations are made up, who belong often to both
classes but who may be found permanently in neither. And this is the element which, as one views it
to-day, ought to give those who think, a cause for
gravest anxiety. For it is a class which reads much,
but not wisely; which is equally open to the social
influences which corrupt it alike from below and from

above; which is most easily fired with discontent, and misled by unbelief, and hardened into practical irreligion. It is the class that is most scantily represented in our churches, and yet without which the Church can do as little as the State. It is the class from which all great reforms have sprung, and in which the religion of the New Testament has found its most courageous champions. When it is said in the gospel, of the Saviour, that "the common people heard Him gladly," what is meant is what we should call the great middle classes. And yet to-day, as one looks down on a great city like this, these are the classes which seem most in danger of settling into a condition of moral insensibility and spiritual apathy.

II. And this brings me to that other question suggested by these tears of Christ. What did they move Him to do? Remember, that so far as the Jerusalem of that day was concerned, He Himself intimates the case to have been hopeless. The insensibility of the generation to which He spoke was impenetrable, and its doom therefore was certain. And yet, amazing folly, as it must have seemed to more than one of those who watched the career of this strange Being, He threw Himself into the work of rousing and alarming Jerusalem, as though its future might instantly be transformed. From the

Mount of Olives He descended straightway to the temple, and the last week of His life was spent in daily intercourse with its chief priests. How vain, as it then appeared, were all His words! How little availed His sternest tones to stir the slumberous pulses of His time. How unmoved (save by a bitter and personal animosity) were the leaders and teachers to whom He spoke. And when that scornful indifference on their part was exchanged at last for a distinctive enmity, with what needless prodigality, as doubtless it seemed even to some of His own disciples, He flung away His life. Flung it away? Aye, but only how soon and how triumphantly to take it again! The defeat of Golgotha meant the victory of the Resurrection. The failure of the cross was the triumph of the Crucified; and though by living and preaching He could not conquer the indifference nor awaken the apathy of Israel, by dying and rising again He did. It was the chief priests who amid the anguish of Calvary were the most scornful spectators and the most relentless foes. It was "a great company of the chief priests," who, on the day of Pentecost, scarce fifty days after that dark and bitter Friday, "were obedient unto the faith." And thus the tide was turned, and though Jerusalem was not rescued from the vandal hordes of Titus, Jerusalem and Judea alike became the home and the cradle of the infant Church.

Such a history is pregnant with lessons for to-day. There are a good many of us, who from the elevation of a thoughtful observation, are looking down on the city in which we live. How fevered and faithless and morally insensible seem multitudes of those who live in it. How can one who loves his fellowmen, who thinks of the possibilities of good as well as of evil that there are in human nature, who sees daily the divine likeness being stamped out of many a young and innocent nature by the coarse and wicked influences that surround it—how can such a one look down on all this and not weep?

God forbid that such a spectacle should leave any one of us insensible or unmoved! But when that is said, let us never forget that with Christ weeping was but the prelude and forerunner of working. There were tears first, but then what heroic and untiring toil! It was not Christ who tired of His work—it was His enemies who tired of Him. And when His work was ended in the flesh, what was that ending but a grander and mightier beginning anew in the spirit! I hear men say that this, and that, and the other endeavor to lift up their fellowmen is a spasm or a failure. I hear them tell their gloomy tales of mistaken endeavors, timidly begun and hastily abandoned. I hear them say, no matter what good cause invites their co-operation, "It is of no use. Most men are bound to go to the devil; it is the part of wisdom to get out of the way and let them go as quickly as possible," and I brand all such cries, no matter in what tones of complacent hopelessness they may utter themselves, as treason against God and slander against humanity! I do not forget how much there is in every individual experience to discourage its hopes for its kind. How many of us here, when we were younger and more sanguine than to-day, have put our hand to some good cause only to find our plans in vain and our efforts wasted. Now when one has reached that point, he is in real and imminent peril, and his peril is this, that he will withhold his hand and withdraw his sympathies from all further co-operation with efforts to lift up his fellowmen, save those which custom enacts, and will wrap himself up in his own plans and interests and let other people take their chances. This is the spirit which when you appeal to it answers, "I will give you something, because you ask me. But I don't believe in your cause, you know. I have been through 'll that. You can not change human nature. And you will only spend your money and your sympathies and your strength in vain." Do you know what that is, my brother? It is paganism, pure and simple! Nay, it is worse than paganism, for even paganism reveals some dumb longing for a lost nobleness and an unrealized ideal. But faithlessness like this is a denial of God, and of goodness as well. And as such,

it is an atheism with which no terms are to be made
nor any truce to be kept. For, high above our blinded
vision there sits One who, as He once wept over
Jerusalem and then died for it, now lives for Jerusalem and for all His wayward children, and who
bids us watch and strive with Him for those for
whom once He shed His blood!

"Careless seems the Great Avenger. History's pages but record
  One death-grapple in the darkness 'twixt old systems and the Word.
  Truth forever on the scaffold,—Wrong forever on the throne,—
  Yet that scaffold sways the future, and, behind the dim unknown
  Standeth God, within the shadow, keeping watch above His own!"

And if He is still watching, even as once He wept
over His creatures, God forbid that of any human soul
you and I should quite despair!

And therefore least of all of our own souls. There
was one characteristic of Christ's tears which can
never be yours or mine. They were unmixed with
any faintest sigh of personal guilt and unworthiness.
How often, on the other hand, is our despair of
others only the echo of those despairing thoughts
which torment us concerning ourselves! How, we
ask, can I be hopeful or strenuous in behalf of other
people when I find so much that is discouraging in
myself? And while I can work for others ("I think,"
wrote a sensitive nature not long ago, "I should go
mad if I could not sometimes forget myself in trying
to do for others"), what can I do for myself? What

can kill in me that coldness which will not feel, that faithlessness that does not pray, that inmost insensibility that can hear about Christ and yet does not love Him?

Such an experience is, I presume, neither exceptional nor uncommon. And yet, how plainly it forgets that power which moved Christ both to weep and to work—that power which, when He went out of the world in the flesh, came back to it in the mission and influence of the Spirit. You and I were made to be inspired just as surely as any ship that ever sailed was made to have her canvas filled with that other rushing mighty wind that thunders above the storm. And so the calling of a life that owns its torpor, its sluggishness, its insensibility, is to put itself in position and open itself to be breathed upon by God. For then, straightway we shall find out what it is to be stirred by a life that gets its mighty pulses straight from the heart of Jesus. And so, while we weep, whether it be over the evil that is in others or in ourselves, our tears will be rainbows, bright with the promise of an immortal hope. Aye, far above the sorrows and the sins of the city that now is, we shall see the splendors of the New Jerusalem that is yet to be. "After this I beheld a great multitude whom no man could number . . . . clothed with white robes and palms in their hands . . . . And he said to me, these

are they that   .   .   .   .   have washed their robes and
made them white in the blood of the Lamb   .   .   .   .
They shall hunger no more, nor thirst any more,   .   .
.   .   for the Lamb which is in the midst of the throne
shall feed them and shall lead them unto living fountains of waters: and God shall wipe away all tears
from their eyes."

SERMON III.

THE CITIZEN'S TWOFOLD STEWARDSHIP.

ST. MATTHEW XXII. 21.

"Render therefore unto Cæsar the things which are Cæsar's; and unto God the things that are God's." *

WE are here this morning in answer to the summons of the civil, and therefore of a secular, authority. We should doubtless keep Thanksgiving Day, — I mean we who are Churchmen, — whether the governor or the president had appointed a day of thanksgiving or not. There is a Thanksgiving Service in the Prayer Book (we have just been using it), and there is a day therein designated for its use. But that day is named with a condition; and that condition is, that some other day shall not have been designated by the civil authority. In other words, the state has had a voice in the ordering of these services, and whatever therefore may be our feeling generally as to speaking in this place of our duties and responsibilities as citizens, it is not easy

---

* New York, Thanksgiving Day, Nov. 27, 1879.

to see how it can be other than appropriate to think of them and to speak of them to-day. Is it said that this is a day for the giving of thanks, and for recounting our mercies? Yes. But it is not impossible that there are some themes for gratitude in connection with our responsibilities to the state and to the nation, an l if so, it is certainly worth while to own and rehearse those responsibilities.

I. But first of all it is important that we do not misunderstand those words in which, in the text, Christ Himself defines a citizen's responsibilities— "Render unto Cæsar the things which are Cæsar's, and unto God the things that are God's." It has not been uncommon to understand this language as if it defined two separate obligations which were in contrast if not in antagonism to one another. The words have been read as if Christ had said: "Here are certain duties which you owe to Cæsar, or to the state. God has nothing to do with those duties (as if God could have nothing to do with any duty!)—but you are to render them because you live in a certain land and under a certain rule. And here, again, are certain duties which you owe to God. Cæsar, or the state, has nothing to do with those duties (as though a state could hope enduringly to prosper and ignore God!)—but you are to render them because you hold a certain religious belief. Now the important thing is that these two duties should be kept distinct, and you must draw a sharp line round each one of them and take care that neither of them becomes confounded with the other." This is Cardinal Manning's doctrine, on the one hand, and the modern pagan's, on the other. Rome says to the state, " Let me alone. It is mine to define morals and duty, and whether my definitions threaten the good order of society and the spread of intelligence and education among the common people or no, you must not interfere." And on the other hand, the modern pagan, who has outgrown God and His law and His gospel, says to the Church, "Let me alone. It is mine to decide what are the duty and obligation of the citizen, whether I seem to you in doing so to threaten the very foundations of all moral distinctions and social order, or not." This has been the controversy which has raged between Cæsarism and Ecclesiasticism through all the Christian centuries, and unlike a great many other controversies, it has raged not because both sides were right, but because both sides were wrong.

Christ is not here defining two duties which were in contrast or antithesis to each other. He is defining one duty, in its just relation to another and a higher duty out of which it grows. Recall the occasion of His words. Some one has brought to Him a penny, and asks Him whether it is lawful for a Jew to pay tribute to a Roman ruler. Says Christ in effect, "My brother, the penny itself has settled that question. It has, stamped upon it, an image or medallion which is Cæsar's likeness. It is current here because this is Cæsar's country, and you use it, whether you choose to own the fact or no, because you are Cæsar's subject. Give Cæsar therefore his due. Pay your taxes, obey the laws, honor the civil authorities; but that you may do so, begin by paying your taxes to God. The penny bears an image; so do you. The penny is from the mint of the emperor; you are from the mint of God. The use of the penny is determined by its likeness. So too, your use is determined by your likeness. Every faculty in you, every gift, every grace and charm and power which is most characteristic and distinctive, is the stamp of the divine. You are God's child. You bear His image. Render to Him your supreme and unceasing tribute; and in doing that, all other and minor questions will settle themselves. 'Render therefore unto Cæsar the things that are Cæsar's,' do I say? Yes. But render them because, and in the inspiration, of that higher duty which bids you render unto God the things that are God's!" It is as though a father should say to his son as the boy turns to leave one of those quiet country homes to which so many hearts revert to-day: You are going, my son, into the strife and bustle and rivalry of a great city. You have chosen to be a merchant. In such a calling you want firmness and diligence, an acute foresight and a vigilant prudence. Give to your calling your best powers. Be a successful merchant, and be an honest man. The cheap contemner of uprightness and integrity will say that the two things are incompatible, but the man who has summered and wintered the street will tell you that, in the long run, the two requirements are one. There may be temporary success and the seeming triumph of brilliant cleverness, without honesty; but in that larger view of affairs which is the only wise view, no success is real or permanent which has not been inspired and controlled by an upright purpose.

And thus we come to understand the meaning of this double precept of the text, and see the way in which, practically, we are to make it real and vital in our lives. More than he is the subject or citizen of any state, is man a citizen and subject of the kingdom of God. And therefore, first of all he is to bring his life under the influence and government of those highest sanctions which come from God. He is to render unto God the things that are God's; and, since all things are God's, he is to consecrate himself and his gifts, first of all, to that highest service, and then, in the spirit of that consecration, he is to do his duty to the community and the state.

His duty. But what is a citizen's duty, as implied

in the teaching and spirit of the religion of the New Testament? I may not undertake to define it in detail, but plainly it is in his dealings with his fellow-citizens, with the commonwealth, and with the nation, to illustrate that peculiar spirit which is the distinctive characteristic of Christ and His religion. That characteristic is not its courage in rebuking wrong, nor its justice in dealing with sin, nor its explicitness in defining the divine authority of the personal conscience and moral truth, though all these are in it; but in one word, in its unselfishness. Looking back over the ministry of Christ and His apostles this is the one principle that interprets the whole. These men and their Divine Leader were burning and throbbing with what the author of "Ecce Homo" has called the enthusiasm of humanity. They saw in their fellows not the actual but the ideal man. They saw in the meanest and guiltiest wretch that lived possibilities of the divinest graces that human character can illustrate. And when they went out from the presence of their Master they went with the determination to make the world better and nobler and happier by what they should do for it. We have a phrase by which we describe one who, in any community, is not so entirely engrossed with his own affairs but that he has some time for the happiness and well-being and advancement of his neighbors, of his city, of his land. We call such a man a pub-

lic-spirited citizen. The early disciples of the religion of Christ were the most public-spirited citizens
whom the world has known. They could think of
something besides their own gain or comfort or advancement; and they not only thought but acted. Is
there any thing else which, in our relations to this
community or to the land, we more urgently need
to-day? It is said that we New Yorkers are conspicuously destitute in what is called the spirit of
civism. We love New York and are proud of it, as
we have a right to be. There is something very
noble and princely in the way in which, on occasion,
the wealth and intelligence and moral force of this
community can weld themselves together and make
of that triple power a weapon with which to wage
war for the integrity of the Union or for the political reform of the metropolis. Like a sleeping giant
New York has tolerated evils, whether within its
own borders or outside of them, of which perhaps
other communities would have been more swiftly
mpatient; but when it has been roused, its wrath
has been terrible, and its energy of reform simply
resistless.

And yet, the charge that, as a community, we are
defective in what the world calls civism is just.
Civism is that spirit or enthusiasm which makes a
man eager to spend and be spent in the service and
welfare of his city. And in this spirit we have by

no means greatly excelled. There have been splendid instances of individual generosity and philanthropy, and the city is adorned and ennobled by their conspicuous fruits. But that co-operative enthusiasm which binds men together in efforts and sacrifices for the public good has been of slow growth and feeble vitality. There are smaller cities in which the public buildings, the museums of art and science and letters are of far nobler proportions and worthier excellence. There have been smaller cities in which the spirit of social and political reform has shown a more vigorous life and a more luxuriant fruitage. It is said that we are too busy to build art museums, and model dwellings for working men, to protect the public parks and gardens, to adorn and beautify our streets and squares. It is said that if men can compound for their lack of personal service by drawing a cheque, there are not many citizens of wealth and character and influence who will not gladly do so. But surely, these are things which ought not to be said. You are to render unto Cæsar the things that are Cæsar's in the spirit of that twin precept which bids you render unto God the things that are God's. Now then, those things in you which are supremely God's, are your powers of generous and unselfish service for your fellowmen. Think what New York might be, if we who live in it would only resolve to construe our obligation of citizenship in no narrow and selfish way! Think of the capital, the energy, the swift and fearless intelligence which throb through all the arteries of our busy and complex life! Who will say if only we could gather up all this wealth and force and cleverness, and bring it to bear even for one day in each week upon the wrongs and evils of our social and municipal life, what revolutions might not be wrought. There are sores in this body politic of ours which are rotting the very bone and sinew of its life. If you want to know what appalling degradation, what nameless vices, what brazen and reckless crime run riot in the very daytime among us, read the last report of the "Society for Improving the Condition of the Poor," and especially so much of it as tells the story of Mr. George Booth's investigations of the homes of the poor. It is a revelation which ought to make every one among us unwilling to sleep in his bed until he has done something to reach and touch and reclaim the lost ones who, within our own precincts, are already fallen into the very pit of damnation, the very crater of hell!

But what has all this, it may be asked, to do with Thanksgiving Day? This is a day not for mourning, but for gratitude. Yes, verily, but it is also a day for reminding ourselves of those ways in which gratitude may find its visible and substantial expression. It is well that we lift here our hearts and voices in common utterance of our grateful praises; but, as

between a gratitude which sings hymns and a gratitude which does something to lift up a fellow man;
there can be no question which is the better. For
myself, I can not conceive any thing more appropriate to this day than that we should ask ourselves,
"How can I translate the gratitude that glows in
my heart this morning, into beneficent and public-
spirited service for my fellowmen? I have a peace-
ful and well-ordered home. I shall sit down, to-day,
to an abundant and well-spread board. Kindred and
friends will gather to brighten these holiday hours
and to make me forget for a little the strifes, the
selfishness, and the sorrows of life." Such thoughts
will surely be in a great many hearts to-day. And
I am very confident that they will kindle at least a
transient glow of gratitude in even the least devout
breast among us. But is not that the truest gratitude
which strives to widen the horizon of human happiness, and to make our fellows sharers in that which
has gladdened us?

And all this has a special and exceptional appropriateness to the circumstances in which we find
ourselves this morning. After a long period of
commercial depression and stagnation, the sky has
begun to clear. The aspect of our commercial life
reminds us of what one may see in summer-time
among the hills, after a long and unbroken drought.
There comes a day when the heavens empty their

treasures among the mountain springs, and set in motion the tiny rills that feed the mountain brooks. And then, if you will take your stand below these upper sources of refreshment, you may see the beds of streams on every hand transformed, as though by a magician's wand. The long dry water-courses, silent and parched and empty, thrill and glow with life. The silver threads that glisten here and there awaken into song. And out of the old and withered slumber of its death, somehow, the land has wakened into life again. Such a spectacle one seems to see as he looks abroad, to-day. The long silent factories hum once more with life and toil. The empty rooms, no longer empty, toss their shuttles to and fro with swift and steady rhythm. The forges and furnaces whose fires had been long dead, whose workmen scattered, gather their toiling throngs once more, and fill the air with the roar of their fierce heats and the jar of their mighty hammers. As the flying car whirls us across some teeming valley after nightfall, we catch the glow of busy industries for which the day is all too short. The land is awake again. The street resumes the aspect of its former throng and feverish impatience. The merchandize of two worlds chokes our railways and crowds our wharves and shipping. Credit, that subtle, sensitive thing, which shrivels before the winds of adverse fortune with such mysterious suddenness, despite the wrongs which "wolves" and gamblers perpetrate in its name, surely and steadily revives.

And all this awakening of traffic, and revival of industry, and return of confidence, redounds in some way to the benefit of each one of us. We are spending more money than we did a year ago, because we are having more money to spend. We are spending money for other and less necessary things than we did a year ago, and expecting to spend still more. Let us be sure that we do so! We want indeed a large element of frugality and forecast in our relations to money; but when we have duly recognized that fact, let us remember that the old-stocking philosophy is as false in finance as it is in religion. It is our talent in action, in circulation, not wrapped up in a napkin, that will bless and help the world, and bless and ennoble ourselves; and that rule holds good whether our particular talent happens to be culture, or the genius of organization, or the gift of sympathy, or the stewardship of money.

But when once that principle is understood and owned, there comes the question, "How, and in what proportions are we spending our money? We have more money to spend than we had last year. How then does it appear? Does it appear only in the fact that we have multiplied our equipages and are more frequently seen in places of public amusement, and are more conspicuous for the splendor of our own

and our children's apparel? We are heartily interested, we say in every kind of good work. How far
does that interest appear in the substantial help that
we contribute to the support of those good works?
What, in one word, is the law of proportion between
what we spend upon ourselves, on our families, and
what we spend, I do not say merely for the poor, but
for the higher interests of our neighbors—for art and
science and the elevation of the unfortunate and the
rescue and regeneration of the spiritually lost? The
coins have begun to flow back again into our hands.
The golden eagle with outstretched wings (apt symbol of the two oceans, whose restless waves forever
challenge the winds, and which bound our continent
on either hand), is a more familiar vision to some of
us on the coinage of our country, than it used to be.
On what gracious errands are we sending those
minted treasures forth again? It is a significant
fact that that particular thing in connection with
which Christ laid down the principle of the text,
"Render unto Cæsar his own, and do it in the spirit
which first renders unto God His own," was a piece
of money. Verily, there could have been no fitter
symbol of His meaning! Money is, in the use men
make of it, the final touchstone of character. Tell
me how a man uses coin or currency, and I will tell
you what he is. It is said that Agassiz could take a
single bone and from it construct in his imagination

or draw out upon the blackboard the whole image of the fish or reptile, of which once it formed a part. Suppose, now, that our money could take on the image of that spirit in which we spend it and of those uses to which we put it; could not one discover the moral structure of a man from looking at a few specimen pieces of this character-currency? And if all the money that is in circulation in the world, to-day could take on the image and superscription of those uses and aspirations with which it was expended, what a revelation of human nature it would be!

And yet, it need not be altogether an unwelcome and humiliating revelation. If you and I, standing in the mint in Philadelphia, should watch the stream of virgin gold as it comes forth for the first time from that complex and beautiful machinery that makes of it the coinage of a nation, it would be almost impossible not to fancy the various errands on which those winged messengers of gold would straightway fly. The mind would conjure up the haunts of trade, the homes of luxury, the dens of vice into which, sooner or later, they will surely find their way. As we heard the ring of their steady fall, as they dropped one by one from the mouth of the machine which had stamped them, the sound would seem to be the echo of that other ring with which they would be flung down in the service of extravagance, of reckless spec-

ulation, or of guilty and shameless indulgence. But
would we not also hear the ring of other coins hallowed to a higher use, sent it may be to some far-off
home of penury and sickness, where old age was
wasting to its end, and where no friendly ministries
smoothed the pathway of indigent refinement to its
grave? Would we not think of museums opened, of
schools builded, of widows comforted, of little children taught and sheltered, of pagan ignorance redeemed and enlightened, by the loving consecration
to their service of other golden messengers? And
whose image, may we be sure, could we look at the
coinage of a Christian country with that closer vision
which detects its spiritual significance, would be
stamped upon the gold and silver which had been
scattered thus? Not ours, brethren, though ours may
have been the sacred privilege of stewardship—not
ours, but Christ's, to whom we have been willing to
consecrate our gains, and in whose fear we have spent
them, whether upon others or upon ourselves.

I do not forget, however, that with many of us
the stewardship of money is not our chiefest stewardship, and that when we come to such a coinage
there are some of us who have little or nothing to
put in circulation. Has the precept of the text or
the incident of its utterance, lost, therefore, all significance for us? On the contrary, if we can not
greatly circulate the currency that buys and sells,

let us remember that ours it still is to circulate the
far mightier currency that cheers and inspires and
consoles. I do not undervalue the power and helpfulness of money. But the world, to-day, is waiting
for something besides money. It is waiting for love
and thought and personal interest and pains-taking.
New York does not so much want great endowments
whether for philanthropy or religion, as it wants the
heart and the brains and the time of busy men who
have now, as they think, no leisure to remember their
citizenship, because they are so swallowed up and
engrossed in interests that are purely personal. Such
an awakening as we witnessed here, last winter, in
the interests of better homes, not for the few but for
the many, reveals what an enormous power for good
there is in a community like this when once it is
roused and stirred to action. It is such personal
action and individual interest that we, most of all,
are waiting for; and therefore whether you are a
capitalist or a clerk, a student or a teacher, a professional man, or a woman living in the retirement
of your kindred and home, take your slumbering
sympathy (I will not believe that God has not im-
planted it within you!) and coin that into love and
service for your kind. On your brow rests the stamp
of Him whose coinage and currency you are. There
are lost pieces of silver, aye, and of gold, which also
bear His image. They have long ago been missing

from the Father's treasury, and are trampled under
foot of man and beast alike. But, if you can find
them in the mire, if you will wash them with your
tears, and burnish them back to brightness and beauty
by your patient and loving touch, you will find on
them the image of Him who made them and the
superscription of His immortal kingdom. Light the
candle of your love then, and sweep diligently till
you find them. Think of some one, to-day, whose
life is lonely, whose youth is gone, whose lot is hard
and cheerless and unlovely, and try to lift them up,
at least for the hour, into the atmosphere of a warmer
and more beneficent brotherhood. Thanksgiving Day
is a good day to go to the hospitals and homes and
refuges and asylums, and to say a cheery word and
reach out a kindly grasp to that most pitiable of all
classes—the people who have no homes. Give up the
theatre and the park and the club, for one afternoon.
Nobody will greatly miss you if you stay away from
these, and some sad faces will kindle into unwonted
sunshine if you turn your steps to-day toward them.
Think of your duties to your city, to your country,
to your fellowmen, and to your God. There has
been a time in your past, unless your lot has been
different from most people's, when things were very
dark with you. You had forgotten Whose you were
and Whom you ought to have served, and when the
blow came, your wasted past rose up before you and

rebuked you with its memories. Did you not resolve, then, that if God should once more be gracious to you, and give you back your old prosperity and happiness, you would be more mindful of His will and more loving toward His children? Have you kept that resolution? Go forth from these walls, resolved that you will keep it to-day. Said one, in old time, to whom God had been gracious, "I will go into thine house with burnt-offerings, and (when I go out again) I will pay thee my vows which I promised with my lips, and spake with my mouth when I was in trouble." May God give to you and me, David's grateful memory and David's steadfast purpose!

SERMON IV.

THE HOMES OF THE POOR.

ST. LUKE X. 32.

"And likewise a Levite, when he was at the place, came and looked on him and passed by on the other side." *

IT was the characteristic criticism of an eccentric divine, that there were a good many occasions in his own life when he found himself in something very like sympathy with this Levite. He took, I presume, that kindlier view of the Levite's character (from which there is nothing in Christ's parable that shuts us out), which sees in him a well-intentioned but inefficient person; and his notion, doubtless, was, that when the Levite, on his way to Jericho, finds his wretched fellow-countryman, robbed, wounded, and half dead, by the roadside, he crosses over to observe him more closely, with a genuine . impulse of sympathy and compassion. Nay, more: that when he finds the dismal extremity of the situation, he turns away, not because he has no pity, but because the circumstances that excited it appear to him so utterly hopeless. The traveller is all but dead.

---

* New York, Feb. 23d, 1879.

To move him may hasten his end. The ghastly wounds out of which his life is slowly ebbing would be closed, if closed at all, too late. The man might die on his hands, and then how could he prove that he had not killed him in a quarrel, or robbed and murdered him himself? It was very dreadful; but, what could one do? It was a case beyond cure, and one could only acknowledge its hopelessness and leave the victim to his fate.

There are a great many situations in life in which one seems almost shut up to the same conclusion. There are evils and miseries that we are all conscious of, that are like the habit of drunkenness. Alcoholism ultimately undermines, often, the whole moral character. There is no meanness that its victim will not resort to, there is no falsehood that he will not utter, in order to gratify his inordinate craving for drink. And in such a case we are tempted to say, "It is no use. There is no sense of shame to appeal to. There is no sentiment of honor to confide in. The man is a moral wreck. How dreadful it is!—and, how hopeless! We will go and look at him; but nothing remains to us after that but to leave him to his fate and pass on."

It is of such an evil that I have been asked to speak to you to-day—an evil at which, many of us, like the Levite, have looked, and then have turned away from, not because we did not deplore it, not because we would not gladly have put our hands to some endeavor for its remedy, but because the situation has seemed to us so hopeless, and the chances of effectual relief so dismally remote. Let me explain why I refer to it this morning.

A few weeks ago, a number of clergymen, including ministers of every denomination, were invited to meet at the house of a gentleman in this city and hear from those who were thoroughly acquainted with them, of the condition of the tenement houses in New York. It was a somewhat unusual occasion. The clergy were the congregation, and, with one or two exceptions, laymen were the preachers. It is fair to the clergy to say that they were a very attentive, and, in many instances, a thoroughly amazed body of listeners. For the facts which they heard were of a character equally startling and appalling. It belongs to this occasion that I should briefly recall them.

There are living in New York to-day more than one million people—the precise figures as closely as ' an be ascertained are one million ninety-seven thousand five hundred and sixty-three. Of these there are one hundred and twenty-five thousand children under five years of age. The total number of deaths last year was twenty-seven thousand and eight, or twenty-four per thousand; this death-rate being twenty-five per cent higher than in Philadelphia. Of the whole number of deaths forty-six per cent (or nearly half) were those of children under five years of age, and of this number of deaths seventy per cent (or nearly three fourths) occurred in, or in connection with, tenement houses. Finally, the number of people living in tenement houses is estimated at five hundred thousand, or at least half of our whole population.

But what is a tenement house? The law defines it as "a house occupied by more than three families living independently and doing their cooking on the premises." This definition would of course include what are known as apartment houses. But a tenement house is a very different thing from an apartment house. Ordinarily it is from four to six stories high, having frequently a shop on the first floor, which, when used (as is often the case) for the sale of liquor, has an entrance from the hall-way so that it can evade the Sunday law and give secret access to the inmates of the tenement at all times. Four families occupy each floor, and a set of rooms consists of one or two dark closets used as bedrooms, and a living room twice as long as one of these pews and ten feet wide. The stair-case is generally dark and the rooms almost entirely without ventilation. This would be a serious evil if they were used for storing hides or tobacco, but the extent of that evil becomes apparent when we remember that in some of these houses occupying a lot twenty-

five feet by a hundred, or just such a lot as an ordinary family of ten or fifteen persons resides upon,
there are often crowded together from ninety to one
hundred and eighty souls. In other words, from four
to nine persons occupy each apartment. Now an
apartment consists ordinarily in such cases of two
rooms. One of these, in which all the cooking and
washing is done, is the living-room—which is dining-
room, sitting-room, parlor, laundry, kitchen, store-
room, and nursery, all in one; and the other is a
sleeping-room, perhaps twice as large as an ordinary
double bed, in which from three to five persons of
both sexes and of all ages, old and young, sick and
well, parents and children, the guest and the lodger,
if there be one, all sleep together. In one of these
lodging rooms the proprietor, who lets lodgings, re-
ceives from eight to twelve lodgers a night, and the
room is fourteen feet long and ten feet wide.

Let us suppose, now, that the hundred or more
persons living in such a house (in one case, at least,
there have been as many as one hundred and eighty-
two) should all be persons of excellent moral training,
with fixed habits on the side of virtue, temperance,
and self-restraint;—it requires no very vivid imagination to picture the miseries of their condition. Of
course, for no single one of them could there be the
smallest chance of privacy. If they were godly people there would never be a moment, night or day,

when they could be secure of even the briefest space
for retirement and devotion. Their life, year in and
year out, must be lived in the continual presence
of others. And even if they were people without
any devout instincts, they would at least be people
with an innate impulse of modesty and reserve.
Think of the torture to a young girl of maidenly
sensitiveness (let us think of it, we whose lives are
hedged about with every circumstance that fosters
such a sentiment) in an existence without privacy,
nay, with the most odious and humiliating publicity.
What are the chances that a pure instinct, that a
modest decorum, that a quick and virtuous sensibility
will long survive, where all the conditions of one's
being systematically conspire to destroy them? Alas,
they do not survive! The class that live in our tenement houses too soon and too largely pass out of the
fellowship of those with whom purity and decency and
morality are possible things. I do not say, that godly
and virtuous men and women do not live in our tenement houses. Thank God! there are many who do!
but when they do, it is because very often they
have survived a moral martyrdom beside which the
triumphs for which the early church canonized St.
Anthony and Perpetua grow pale and dim.

For, in order to appreciate the situation of our
tenement house population, you must add to the inevitable evils that come from over-crowded, ill-venti-

lated, viciously-arranged apartments, those others that come from intemperance and crime and neglect. Over against this wretched life, so scanty and so uninviting in its home-aspects, stands the gin-palace and the corner grocery, in which heartlessness and greed conspire to demoralize the parents and rob the children. An incident like this is a sample of the infernal spirit which still has its way in this city with but scant restraint. A laboring man out of work took to drink. He had no money, but the rum-seller, in spite of the remonstrances of the man's wife, sold him what he wanted on credit. Meantime the rum-seller's wife employed the laborer's wife to do plain sewing for her, and when the week's work was done, instigated by her husband, she withheld the money due, claiming it as a debt owed to the rum-seller for liquor furnished to the man whose heroic wife was thus striving to support herself and her children. Fortunately, the law was equal to the emergency in this instance; but in hundreds of others just as monstrous it is not. And as a consequence, side by side with all the evils inseparable from over-crowded tenements there reign unchecked those other evils which are the fruit of wide-spread intemperance and its consequent vice and crime.

And so it comes to pass that there are men and women, aye, and children, too, living in this New York of ours, who are gradually losing all trace of the

humanity with which God endowed them. The instincts that are coarsest and most brutal—those that
ally them most closely to the savage and the animal,
—these are the only instincts that, in a little while,
survive. It is not long since a woman was found dead,
—destroyed by vice and drink,—in one of these tene
ment houses, with her children playing as unconcern-
edly around her dead body as though it had been a
graven image. What did they know about mother-
love? What experience had they in the tenderness
and care that make that word the synonym for every
thing that is sweet and gracious? To eat and sleep
and wallow in the filth in which they had been born
and nurtured, this was all that they knew of life. And
when such children grow up, what has the community
to hope—or rather, what has it not to fear from them?
"It has truly been said," wrote Mr. Edward Crapsey in
an invaluable series of papers published some seven
years ago in the *Galaxy* under the title of "The
Nether Side of New York,"—"It has truly been said
that the home is the last analysis of the state; and it is
not strange that the civic virtues decay in a community
where, in any true sense of the word, one half of the
people have no home at all. The profligacy of New
York, after allowance has been made for the gross ex-
aggerations due to partisan rancor, is considerable and
shameful; but, resting as the city does upon this tenement system, it is wonderful that it retains so much

of physical and moral vitality. Family privacy, which is the foundation of public morality and intelligence, is within the reach of but a small fraction of the population. . . . . . . In a sanitary sense the tenements are a perplexity and a vexation; but it is in their moral and social aspects that they are perilous. There are hundreds of these immense barracks in which from fifteen to fifty families live under one roof, using halls, staircases, closets, and all the conveniences for the privacy of life in common. In every one of these families there are females of course, and there are very few in which there are not children as well. No truth is more universally recognized than that barrack life is demoralizing even in the army; and remembering this fact, some idea of its destructive influences when it is inflicted upon a half million of men, women and children can readily be formed. With half its population camped in its heart, the city has, to the reflective publicist who traces effects to their first cause, a disheartening future. The first generation of tenement life has already destroyed, in a great measure, the safeguards which a genuine home erects around a people, and it is simply inevitable that in the second or third generation it must brutalize its victims and leave vice and ignorance as the foundation stones of the municipality."*

"The Nether Side of New York," by Edward Crapsey, pp. 115-116. Sheldon & Co.

But at this point it may be asked, "Why do I speak of these things in this place and on this day? Doubtless the condition of those who live in tenement houses is wretched enough, and the future of a city which endures them is gloomy enough, but after all, such questions are philanthropic rather than religious,—a matter for the humanitarian rather than for the Christian. It may be well for us to walk across to the east side of the town and, like the Levite, look at our unhappy brother, fallen by the wayside, and worse than wounded and half dead; but the case is almost a hopeless one, and if it be not, it is not for us to consider it here. The Church exists in the interests of religion. Religion exists to show us how, in this world, to get ready for another. It exists to awaken sinners and to edify believers, and to comfort the sorrowful, and to speak words of hope and consolation to the mourner. It is a mistake when ministers turn aside from their proper work to give attention to these humanitarian schemes. Let them preach the gospel, and visit their people, and administer the Sacraments, and leave these outside interests to those who, having no gospel to preach, must needs supply its place with some philanthropic or humanitarian substitute. The Church was not organized to build model tenements, nor to diffuse sounder schemes of drainage or ventilation. Whenever it comes down from its high level, and turns aside from its more sacred functions, it forgets its dignity, and jeopardizes its influence.

Somebody has said, in answer to such sentiments, that when men or institutions reach that point when they are chiefly concerned about conserving their dignity and their influence, they are very close to that period when they will cease to have either to conserve. Whether that be true or no, I am very sure that the Church was not organized to be chiefly concerned about watching her reputation or nursing her influence. As little, undoubtedly, was she organized to build model tenements and to organize stock-companies for the inauguration of a better system of drainage. Her kingdom is not of this world, and whenever she has undertaken to immerse herself deeply in secular affairs she has been more in danger of the secular spirit than even men of the world themselves. For one, I should not consider it a blessing, but an evil, if a capitalist should offer this parish a million of dollars on condition that it expended that sum in rearing model dwellings for the poor and working classes, and assumed the business of their management. Managing real estate is not the calling of the Church, and few institutions are so poorly adapted for such a task as would be a parish or congregation.

But managing real estate is the business of the individual citizen, and as to the moral bearings of that or any other earthly business, the Church, as the witness and messenger of an eternal moral Governor, nay, as the messenger, most of all of a God once incarnate in our common humanity, must needs, if it has any business at all in the world, have a good deal to say. I wonder if those who would so sharply confine the Church and the ministry to certain official and ceremonial functions, have ever read the New Testament. We may take the ministry of Christ, I suppose, as at once a prophecy and pattern of what the work and ministry of the Church should be to-day. But Christ did not merely preach the Sermon on the Mount and die on the cross. There was no disease so loathsome that He did not put forth His hand and touch it. There was no home that He went into, whether it was the home of that Pharisee whose dirty inhospitality He gently rebuked for giving Him no water wherewith to wash His feet, or the home of Simon's wife's mother, which He did not leave until He had expelled the fever which poisoned it and her;—there was no home, I say, which Christ entered, so far as we have any account of His ministry, which He did not leave, both physically and morally, sweeter and decenter and purer because He had entered it. And what He did, to the lame and the blind and the halt and the leper and the impure and the morally vile, I suppose that you and I who profess to be, in one sense or another, His baptized disciples, may wisely be concerned about doing also!

" Preach me a comforting sermon, O pastor ! " cries some one to whom apparently religion exists to stir the emotions, and give one the comfortable glow of an unwonted excitement. Believe me, the Church of God in this generation has a much more serious business than the business of preaching comforting sermons. It has been dealing, of late, so much in what one has called not too strongly " the mush of emotionalism " that it is a grave question with some whether the moral fibre has not altogether gone out of it. It is time that it was understood, that in a sense more real and critical than ever before in this land, religion is on trial among us. Men are asking,— and they are not all revolutionists either,— " For what does the Church exist among us ? Why is it ex- empted from taxation ? " One of the worst tenement houses in New York was once a church, and passed from its sacred uses to those which now make it a blight and curse upon the community. If the Church is to be exempt from taxation, she ought to be mak- ng some sort of return for such exemption; and if, in view of the situation in this city to-day, she is dumb and silent,—if she has no warning to utter, and no plain facts to hold up to men who frequent her courts,—then it is a very grave question whether she has not outlived her usefulness.

For what is, or ought to be, the burden of her message ? Is it not that God is the Father of all His

children, and that, in Christ, humanity was meant
to be one loving and self-forgetting brotherhood?
Is it not that, in the shadow of that exceeding compassion which poured itself out on the cross, you and
I were meant to learn a lesson of equal compassion
for every sin and sorrow-burdened nature, and to
illustrate that compassion by the eagerness and the
helpfulness with which we reach out to help and rescue those who are less favored than ourselves? God
forbid that we should forget the Church's function
as the witness to an immortal hope, and the teacher
of an abounding consolation! But God forbid, no less,
that we should forget her function to tell men to do
justly and to love mercy, and, in the daily business
of the week, to seek those things which lift men up,
and not to be content—no! not for one instant to be
content,—with those things that pull them down, and
degrade and everlastingly destroy them!

As to the best method of grappling with the evil
which exists in the present homes of the poor, this
is not the place to speak. The problem is a large
one, and no one solution will fit every emergency and
overcome all obstacles. I must confess my own sympathy with the plan adopted by Miss Octavia Hill
in London, where that remarkable woman, aided by
Mr. Ruskin, took a row of tenement houses of very
inferior character and gradually reformed and im-
proved them, by invoking, from the start, the sym-

pathy and co-operation of the inmates. Undoubtedly
no old houses, defective in construction and arrange-
ment, can be made so wholesome and convenient as
those built to-day with special reference to light
and ventilation and drainage, and the avoidance of
over-crowding. But, on the other hand, no tenement house, however admirable its construction, will
benefit its inmates until they themselves have been
taught how to live in, and care for it. What the
poor want is education conveyed with sympathy.
What they do not want are condescension and alms.
They are quick enough to know the difference between people who are in accord with them, and
those who are simply doing what they do for them
as a sop to their own consciences. And no sign in
our mission-work in New York is more hopeful than
the abundant indication there is that that work is
being recognized as something more than preaching
on Sunday morning and holding a Sunday-school on
Sunday afternoon. I wish that those among us who
have never seen it would visit the Kindergarten at
Olivet Chapel in whose good work this congregation
has been for some time most efficiently represented,
and where the children of the poor are given object
lessons in those domestic duties which have so much
to do with the comfort of the house. The work which
Miss Juliet Corson is doing in connection with an association of ladies, in teaching the poor how to cook

cheaply and palatably, is in the same admirable direction, as is also the instruction given in the Wilson Industrial School, and the influence of such an institution as our own Day-Nursery. All such agencies conspire to teach those who sorely need the lesson, how much cleanliness, orderliness, modesty, and a wise economy, have to do with the happiness and healthfulness of life; and for such a work we may well thank God and take courage.

But behind the training which we give the children of the tenement houses when, for a few hours, we draw them out of them, lies the influence of their homes when they return to them. We must learn to follow them there. Sooner or later, if society is not to be split squarely into two hostile and mutually destructive factions, we must gather up the torn ligaments of alienated sympathies and somehow reknit and revivify them. "The people's homes are bad," writes Octavia Hill in her volume on the *Homes of the London Poor*, "partly because they are badly built and badly arranged; they are tenfold worse, because their habits and lives are what they are. Transplant them, to-morrow, to healthy and commodious homes and they would, in many instances, pollute and destroy them. There needs, and will need for some time, a reformatory work which will demand that loving zeal of individuals which can not be had for money, and can not be legislated into existence by parliament.

The heart of the English nation will supply it, individual, reverent, firm, and wise." So speaks an Englishwoman's faith in her own countrymen. I have a faith no less hearty in what can be done, if they but choose, by the Christian men and women of New York. One of the latter, the wife of a physician residing in the lower part of the city, has already shown us what even one woman can do in lifting up the poor, and in thus lifting up their homes with them.

Meantime it will be a blessed thing if Christian capitalists, men without too eager an eye to pecuniary profit, build at least one block of houses for working men, which should be, in every respect, a model for such constructions. One such norm or type of what a tenement house ought to be, would be a boon of inestimable value, and of wide and most wholesome influence.

But whatever methods we may employ to lift up our brother, fallen and perishing by the way, may God give us patience and courage and hope! May He help us to remember Whose we are, and Whose they are, who are huddled in yonder abodes of squalor and misery. I might point out to you the ties that bind you and them together in a common peril, of which, ordinarily, we do not dream. The men-servants and maid-servants in our houses are often the brothers and sisters of the men and

women and children in some crowded tenement.
When you wonder how the fatal fever found its
way into your pure and well-ordered home, you do
not remember that the maid who held your child
in her arms, may have been, the evening before,
while clad in the same garments, holding the fever-
tossed child of her brother or sister in the same arms;
and so, may have brought the deadly contagion from
yonder crowded room, miscalled a home, straight to
yours. If you did remember it, perhaps you would
be eager to remedy an evil which threatened so ter-
ribly not only others, but yourself. But such a motive
would be but a poor and ignoble one, at the best.
There is another and a diviner motive. The mother
of that child, my sister, is your sister. His father,
my brother, is your brother. The life of his little
one is not less dear to him than yours to you. God
has given to you something of the ability to save
that life, to redeem and uplift these children of the
common Father, and to make the world somehow
brighter and purer and better for each one of them.
I dare not undertake to say in just which way you
best may exercise that ability. But ask God to show
you the way, and when He has, make haste to follow it!

SERMON V.

THE SOCIAL INDIFFERENTIST.

ACTS XVIII. 17.

" And Gallio cared for none of those things." *

THE things for which Gallio thus cared nothing, were in one sense none of his business. He was the Roman deputy or pro-consul of Achaia, and his official residence, at the time St. Paul visited it, seems to have been at Corinth. As elsewhere, so at Corinth, the ministry of the apostle provoked the enmity principally of his own countrymen. The Greeks heard him, and were attracted to him. The Hebrews heard him, and hated him. And here too, as on other occasions, their hatred took on the form of personal violence. If we were to describe what they did in our own dialect rather than theirs we should say that they mobbed him. With but the slightest warrant of law they rose upon him in the street, dragged him before Gallio, and charged him with being heterodox as a religious teacher. "This fellow persua-

---

* New York, Nov. 23, 1878.

deth men to worship God contrary to the law"; by which they meant their law,—the Jewish law.

With such a question Gallio had nothing to do. It was not a question of civil or social order, but of theology, and concerning theological differences the empire and its servants had no jurisdiction. Gallio rightly refused to entertain the charge, and promptly dismissed the complaint. But this was not the end. The Greeks had sympathized with Paul. Whether they accepted his teachings or not, they seem on this occasion to have believed in the right of free speech, and, like a great many other champions of free speech, they proceeded to proclaim their sympathies by an act of personal violence. The most active individual in the assault and arrest of St. Paul, had been a man named Sosthenes, the ruler or rabbi of the synagogue. He was, by virtue almost of his position, a religious zealot, and he hated the apostle with a hatred which was not the less virulent because it was professional. He had doubtless incited the mob and had suggested the arrest. And so when the Greeks see that Gallio refuses to sustain him in a proceeding so high-handed, and indeed refuses to give him the smallest countenance, they turn upon this Jewish ecclesiastic with heartiest satisfaction and proceed, in full view of Gallio's judgment-seat, to beat him.

And though the beating was without the smallest

legal warrant,—though it was even a more gross and disorderly breach of the peace than that which had preceded it,—"Gallio cared for none of those things." One can see the Roman quæstor as he lounged in his official chair, and watched the blows and listened to the cries which broke the hot and slumberous stillness of that Asiatic mid-day. These dogs of Jews and these emasculated Corinthians, so long as the peace of the empire was undisturbed, what mattered it how much they quarrelled? He was there to crush an insurrection, if it should arise—to collect and forward the imperial revenues to Rome, and meantime, to dream of the splendors of the capital and—regret them. It was a dreary business, this pro-consular life. The Corinth of that day was but a shrunken memory of the Corinth of other and more prosperous days. Rome was the heart of the world, and as the deputy recalled her princely magnificence and her prodigal luxury (for it was the year that Nero ascended the throne), he turned from the dulness of this official expatriation with mingled impatience and indifference. Did the lictor say there was fighting in the streets? that the Greeks were beating the Hebrews? Well, what mattered it? Who cared? He was very sure that he did not.

This picture of an amiable and cultivated indifferentism may, I think, wisely detain us for a few moments. Its conspicuous characteristic in this particular instance lay in this, that it betrayed such an utter insensibility to the simplest principles of justice. Sosthenes, the Jewish ruler of the synagogue, and his Israelitish companions in Corinth, had undoubtedly done St. Paul a wrong in arresting him and bringing him before the deputy. But they had done that wrong under legal forms, and had appealed to the pro-consul for their authority. The Greeks, on the other hand, had deliberately taken the law into their own hands, and were beating a Jew without the smallest warrant of either law or adequate provocation. Now undoubtedly, in a technical sense, this was no concern of Gallio's. He was sent to Corinth simply to look after the interests of Rome, and there was a certain wisdom in his being officially ignorant of the religious quarrels between Greeks and Jews, whether in Corinth or elsewhere. But, in another and very real sense, his indifference was neither wise nor loyal nor manly.

Amid the civilizations of that day Rome stood conspicuously, as the witness for law and justice. A Roman citizen owed it to his sovereign to be everywhere the friend of fair dealing; and if Gallio had really cared to win for the empire the trust and loyalty of her conquered peoples, he would have seen to it that, so far as he could prevent it, no blow should be unjustly struck, nor any meanest citizen of Corinth, whether Jew or Greek, lightly or lawlessly wronged.

But to have done this would have been to cease to be an official, and to become an enthusiast—a philanthropist; it would have been to break through the crust of that passionless indifference which was the mark of culture in those days, and to allow one's life to be stirred by emotions and touched by sympathies concerning one's fellowmen. And against this, all the past training, the personal habits, the more selfish instincts of the man, with equal earnestness cried out. His culture had made him an indifferentist, and he could not bring himself to consent to be any thing else.

"But that," we say, "was a pagan culture, and its fruit was worthy of the tree. Such a character as Gallio's has a certain historic interest, but beyond that, it is largely without significance. We are not pagans, but Christians, and we are bound inflexibly to repudiate the principles of such a man's career, and the maxims by which he was governed." Yes, verily, we are so bound; but what, let me ask, are the facts? You and I are living in an age, and largely in an atmosphere, of what we call culture. We have been taught to value accomplishments, to cultivate the arts, to cherish and strive after refinement of manners. And in our generation, as a result of such a culture, there is a civilization of a distinctly finer fibre than that which was known to our ancestors. Now one distinguishing mark of that civilization is a development of individual reserve. We learn to conceal emotions, or at least to chasten their expressions. That simple and natural enthusiasm which is the especial characteristic of youth is frowned upon or else ridiculed, until a young girl or a young man with an ardent and glowing interest in any thing or any body is almost a social phenomenon. We have chastened our voices, and our gestures, and perhaps most successfully of all, our nobler and more unselfish impulses. Tell some one a story of wrong, or want, or human sorrow, and the chances are you will get the answer, "Really, how very unpleasant. Can you not find something more agreeable to talk about than that?" There is a shrinking from even the sight of misery, an unwillingness to hear about want or vice or sorrow, which closes sometimes every avenue of approach, and bars the way against every urgency of appeal.

Nor is this wholly surprising; nor indeed altogether without excuse. My neighbor, whose ear is attuned to a sensitiveness of which I can not even conceive, is thrown into a spasm of torture by a musical discord, which my less tutored faculty scarce perceives. It hurts him; and, to leave that fact out of account in judging of the way in which he endures a series of discords, is neither just nor kindly. Now then, it is a result of the complex thing that we call culture, that it makes the sensibilities infinitely more

susceptible to external impressions. Poverty, sickness, the dismal effects of vice and crime, these things
shock and pain a highly trained and therefore a highly
sensitive nature far more than one that is not highly
trained.

And therefore it is not unnatural that such natures
should turn away from pain. It is not surprising that
they are unwilling to hear of the injustices, the hard-
ships, the miseries that are torturing so many of their
fellowmen. Nor is it surprising either, that, refusing
to know about such things, they cease, before long,
to care about them. It is the old picture of Gallio,
watching through the parted drapery the scourging
of Sosthenes in the street. It is not an engaging
spectacle. Here at hand is the last chronicle of the
busy and brilliant life of the capital. Here is the last
roll that has come from the pen of Seneca. Seneca,
as that profane history of the time which throws so
many side lights upon the history of the New Testament tells us, was a kinsman of Gallio. Gallio was
himself, as we learn from the same source, a lover of
letters and of literary men. How much pleasanter
to lose one's self in the pages of Ovid or Lucullus or
Martial instead of going out into the hot sun to stop
a street fight between a herd of fanatical Israelites
and Corinthians! And so, to-day, there is a large
class that finds it far pleasanter to draw the cur-
tains upon the crime and sorrow that are without,

and, with the freshest voice in song or story to beguile them, to forget that there are men and women and children all around them, whose lives are crowded so full of cruelty and penury and vice that, though they are God's children, they themselves do not even dream it.

And yet, fellow men and women of a Christian civilization, how utterly and how amazingly is this to miss the noblest end of culture! The function of culture is not merely to train the powers for enjoyment, but first and supremely for helpful service. I can imagine a physician, gifted with that finer intuition which is often so surprisingly developed by familiarity with disease, who should say to himself, "This gift of mine causes me so much pain that I must really decline to use it. To see, as I must needs see, in an active practice, so many instances where my surer knowledge discerns the dreary and hopeless end all the way from the beginning,—this is a kind of professional experience which costs more than it is worth. I know that this finer sense of mine fits me in an exceptional degree to forecast and so alleviate the sufferings of others. But the process is too disagreeable. I had rather know less, and so care less, because I suffer less myself." I say I can imagine such a case as that, and yet there is not one of us who would not call such a course alike cowardly and selfish. How is it less so, when our culture, which, though it may not have been professional, has educated every faculty in us to a keener and acuter sensitiveness, produces no nobler impulse than the impulse of indifferentism? Is it for this that civilization exists? Is it for this that wealth and education and social refinement and hereditary abilities have made of certain people or classes among us, what we rightly call privileged classes? Above all, is this the end of a culture whose supreme dignity is, or ought to be, that it is a Christian culture? I am not unmindful that there is a considerable school of thinkers and teachers in our day who, while illustrating in many departments of human attainment the finest culture, distinctly repudiate the name of Christian. But you and I do not repudiate it. We are here to-day, because, whether consciously or unconsciously, we recognize that the most helpful element in our moral and social education has come from the religion of Jesus Christ? But what is the religion of Jesus Christ? Is it a ceremony, whether of marriage or burial, of baptism or of communion, or is it something more? We maintain the ceremonies, but we do so, surely not because they are an end, but rather a means to an end. We bring our children to baptism, and come ourselves to confirmation, and to yonder altar. We come and invoke the blessing of Christ and His Church upon what the state calls the merely civil contract of marriage,—we associate our joys and our sorrows, our journeys and our mercies with certain public and solemn services, and why? Is it not to bring Christ into and close to our common life, and so ennoble that life by the sweetness and sanctity which He alone can shed upon it? Is it not that, amid the hopes and the disappointments, the sorrow and the gladness of our earthly lot, He who called Matthew, and praised Nathaniel, and consoled Mary, and forgave Peter, may bless and strengthen us? Would we care to have a culture, a home life, a measurement of time that left out Christmas and Easter and Good Friday and All Saints' Day? "No, surely," I can not doubt that you will say. "We may not have prized the Christian element in our culture as we ought, but God forbid that we should be without it!" And yet, is Christ in the world only to cheer you and me? Shall we selfishly turn to Him to comfort us, and catch no impulse from His life to reach out and comfort our brethren? Did He come only to teach us how to build handsome churches and keep them for ourselves,—to maintain a beautiful and sonorous worship,—to support a dignified ministry who should from time to time lend a kind of sacred *eclat* to the wedding or funeral or other solemnities with which our life is punctuated? Did He,—this Christ who had not where to lay His head, and whose feet and hands were nailed for our salvation to the accursed tree,—did He, think you, hang on a cross and die as a felon, that you and I might at length be dispatched out of this world with a safe and comfortable *viaticum*, and all the while that we stayed in it think of the sorrows and sufferings of our fellowmen only with a careless and easy indifference? For if He did, this at least we may surely say, that the enormous dimensions of His sacrifice were out of all proportion to the pitiful meagreness of its results!

O no, it was not merely for you and me that Christ died, but for humanity. Into the culture of that elder time He came to put the one ingredient that it needed supremely to ennoble it—the ingredient of a divine unselfishness. He came to make hateful and odious that cultivated self-love which cares nothing for another's welfare. He came to kill out that torpid indifference that could see wrong and cruelty and injustice, and "care for none of those things," and to supplant it with an inextinguishable and self-forgetting love. And for such a spirit, our later culture, Christian it may be in name, but pagan too often, I fear, in spirit, no less than that other and elder, waits and aches. Every now and then our ears are startled by some brutal deed, some inhuman cruelty that makes us shudder for our kind. And, reading of it amid our own safe and comfortable surroundings, we cry out, "How shocking! How barbarous! Where were the police!" Verily such an inquiry, nowadays, betrays a sense of humor, if it betrays no more. But if in this or any other community there existed a police with every ideal quality which we are wont to impute to such an agency, it would not at all touch or heal that deadly gangrene which is at the root of all our social evils. At best a municipal discipline, however admirable, can only repress and punish the outward manifestations of our social evils. The medicine that shall heal them must be drawn from that divine fountain which was opened when the Son of man hung dying upon the cross of Calvary. And you and I, the disciples of that Son of man, must be the channels, the living and breathing channels, through which the throbbing tide of sympathy and renewal which flows forth from that fountain, shall reach and heal the sorrows and the sins of our fellows. The other day, in Wales, the waters broke out in a colliery. There were four hundred men at work in the winding drifts far down below the surface, and panic-stricken with the fatal sound, they rushed to the mouth of the pit and touched the telegraphic signal that was placed to tell the watchers, five hundred feet above them, of their dangers. They had scarcely done so when to their horror they remembered that, that morning, the signal-wire had parted, and had not yet been mended. What were they to do? The water was steadily rising, and in a little while their chance of life would be measured not by hours but by minutes. With the energy of despair, one of them, trained at sea, flung himself against the ragged sides of the shaft, and with a grasp that seemed a superhuman endowment given him for the moment, scaled the perpendicular wall until he came to the break in the wire. The parted ends hung within a few inches of each other, but how was he to join them together? To let go his hands and strive to reach them thus was death to himself and death to those below him. Suddenly, with an inspiration born of the dire peril, he grasped one end in his mouth, and reaching then with agonizing effort for the other, caught the two between his lips, reunited thus the parted wire, and re-established the electric current that told up to those above the danger, and signalled swiftly back again the coming of deliverance.

What he climbed up to do, you and I must climb down to do. There is a vast multitude below us that our lips and hands and feet must bring into living and saving relations with the Son of God. To be careless of their well-being, is not merely suicidal in its ultimate results to our own; to be indifferent to the ignorance and vice and crime that are about us, this I say, is not merely to imperil our property and jeopard our personal safety,—such considerations, however fitting elsewhere, are surely scarcely worthy to be urged here,—it is to forget Whose name we profess, and Whose example we are called to imitate. Not to care when the feet of other men and women, no matter how obscure or remote from us, are going down to hell, this, disguise it as we may, is not Christianity, but paganism blank and heartless.

Believe me, such paganism is very full of peril. One does not need to be a pessimist in order to perceive that the social problem now confronting us is one of the gravest and most threatening problems of our time. The laborer does not love the capitalist, and the capitalist does not always understand the laborer. But we shall not finally silence the heresies of the communist with the bullets of the militia. Over against the unreason, the crudeness of thought and the extravagance of speech that fever the life of the working-man, we must rear something better than the stern front of a stony indifference. If his misfortunes are not our fault, none the less he himself is our brother. And somehow—anyhow—we must make him feel that we account him so. It is for this most of all, that we should prize every good work that brings us into personal intercourse with the unfortunate. It brings the parted ends of our great social nerve together. It helps to make Christ real to those who, if they even believe in Him at all, must begin to believe in Him, because they see His divine unselfishness reflected in His disciples. And this is missionary work. It is not the only mission-

ary work that you and I are called upon to do, but
it is the work that lies nearest to us, and closest of
all. Let us be ashamed, then, to be indifferent to it.
If God has given us culture, if he has given us wealth,
or a quick sympathy, or a robust intelligence, or a
persistent will—and to each one of us He has given
one or other of these gifts—let us take and use our
gift for those whose lot is harder and less favored
than our own! If while others have sorrowed and
suffered and sinned we have lounged like Gallio,
"caring for none of those things," let us hearken
Whose voice it is that says, "Ye call me Master and
Lord; and ye say well, for so I am. If I then, your
Lord and Master, have washed your feet, ye also ought
to wash one another's feet. For, I have given you an
example that ye should do as I have done to you."

SERMON VI.

THE PERILS OF WEALTH.

ST. MATTHEW XIX. 24.

"It is easier for a camel to go through the eye of a needle, than for a rich man to enter into the Kingdom of God." *

It has been common, in explaining this language, to understand by the phrase "the eye of a needle," the smaller gate which in Eastern cities admits the foot passenger after nightfall. In the walled towns of the East, the caravan, and of course the camels as a part of it, entered a city by means of the great gates which were wont to be closed at sunset. If one sought entrance later, he must effect it, if at all, through the low-browed portal at one side, through which a man, stooping and dismounted, might just pass; for a camel, encumbered with his hump and his burden, the thing was almost, if not quite, impossible.

This has been one explanation. Another has been to read in place of the word translated "camel" another, closely resembling it, meaning "rope" or "cable," so that the text would run, "It is easier for a rope

---

* New York, Feb. 17, 1878.

or cable to go through the eye of a needle than for a rich man to enter into the kingdom of God."

Of course the effort, in both these new readings, has been to get rid of the idea of absolute impossibility. I do not see that it is successful, even if we accept those readings. For which, in fact, there is but doubtful authority. Soften the figure as you may, it presents to men of wealth a most discouraging prospect. It was meant to. If he approaches it on the basis of his wealth, no rich man can enter into the kingdom of God. Christ declines to know him on any such terms. Going back a few verses we find the occasion of this tremendous language in that most affecting interview of Christ with a rich young man. This youth, with a sensitive conscience, with a stainless reputation, with a thoroughly awakened interest, comes to Jesus, asking, "Master, what good thing shall I do that I may have eternal life?" Christ answers him, "If thou wilt enter into life, keep the commandments." Says the young man, "I have kept them from my youth up. What lack I yet?" "This," answers Christ in substance, "the temper that counts property worthless beside true life. You come to me with your money, with your sense of complacency, of consequence, of power, and you want to bring these with you into the kingdom of God. You are not indeed satisfied with things as they are. How can you be, so long as you are vainly striving to feed your immortal nature upon husks and chaff? You want to be enlarged into a life nobler, fuller, worthier of your better self. But you would come as Dives, not as Lazarus. What you have, ought, you think, to be reckoned in with what you are. You and your estate are in your own conception too entirely identified to be separated. Believe me, my young brother, the kingdom of Jesus can not know you upon any such terms. It is not necessary that you should be stripped bare of all your belongings in order to enter it. But you should be willing to be stripped bare. You must come to look upon what you call yours as though it mattered not, when you set your face toward the kingdom of God, whether it were yours or no. The spirit of renunciation must be so deep in you that, with the apostle, you must be ready to "count all things but lost, that you may win Christ and be found in Him." And this not from any arbitrary reason, but simply because a human heart is not large enough to hold two thrones. If Christ is to be in it at all He must be King of the whole domain; and if He is to be King, the money power, the sense power, the brain power must go to the rear. There will be a place for each of these in every sanctified life, but it must be a subordinate place. "Go," or at least, if it be a question between your securities and your Saviour, be ready to go, "and sell all that thou hast, and follow me!"

It is of this personal interview that the text and the context are the summing up. As I began by saying commentators have tried with futile ingenuity, and with very indifferent success, to soften it. I do not wonder. Wealth is, or seems to be, such a considerable power in the world; the Church has tried so hard in so many ages to acquire it and to wield it, the ongoing of philanthropic enterprises and of advancing civilization appear to be so largely dependent upon it, that there is a continual temptation in speaking to men of wealth to soften such language or to overlook it.

Let us not, in shunning that danger, exaggerate or over-state it. The possession of riches is fraught with peril. But it does not follow therefore that the possessor of riches is to renounce them. The rich man is exposed to a danger from which the poor man is happily free. But it is not to be hastily concluded from this that the rich man is to give all that he has to the poor. Wealth has duties to perform in the constitution of our modern society, that poverty could never perform. The progress of science, of the arts, of higher education, the organized efforts of philanthropy, require capital in the hands of a few, just as truly as trade requires capital. And wealth thus used by the wealthy becomes a permanent and inestimable factor in the elevation of men. Nay, more, if in deference to any narrow and superficial interpretation of Christ's language, a man should take his wealth and distribute the whole of it in largesses to the poor to-morrow, he would be doing the poor an incalculable evil and not a benefit. Men ask, "Why do not you, as a believer in Jesus Christ and the Sermon on the Mount, make common cause in the things of this world with the destitute around you, and trust for the needful food and raiment to Him who feeds the birds and clothes the lilies?" Why not, indeed? Is it merely because such an act would be fanatical or enthusiastic, or because political economy forbids it? Or, because, whatever else I ought or ought not to do, I ought not to do my brother man a wrong? Is any body ignorant of the fact that every human life needs the discipline of forethought and self-denial, of responsibility and self-help, and that if I by my ill-judged kindness enable another to escape these things I am degrading and hurting him as well as abusing my own power? What would be the effect of the announcement that half a dozen rich men had disinherited themselves, and that to-morrow morning fifty millions of dollars would be distributed to the poor? Does any body care to contemplate the pandemonium that New York would become—the idleness, the licentiousness, the fierce hatreds, the bitter discords, the mad license that would be engendered: and ought a Christian man to do an act that would make his brother men incalculably worse instead of better?

No, the possession of wealth is not inconsistent with our Christianity nor alien from it. We turn from words of Christ which seem, if we rest in the letter and do not go beneath the letter to their spirit, to read so like the teachings of our modern communism and we come straightway in apostolic history to a condition of society precisely like our own. "Charge them that are rich in this world," writes an apostle, and we know straightway, that in that early fervor of the infant faith there were rich men in the Church of God as well as poor men. Nay, how can we pretend to ignore them, men and women as well, when we recall Jairus, and Cornelius, Zacchæus, and Joseph of Arimathea, Acquila and Priscilla, Dorcas and Lydia, the hospitable and generous Publius in the Island of Malta, Rufus and Gaius the princely freemen of Rome, and Erastus the chamberlain in the imperial household? If, in those early days, not many wise, not many mighty, not many noble, were called, the Church nevertheless gathered to the feet of its Master wealth as well as poverty—wealth that was ready to part with all if need be, rather than be parted from Christ, but wealth that, nevertheless, its possessors were permitted to keep if only they were mindful of its perils.

If only they were mindful of its perils, I say, and the question for us is, Whether those perils have ceased? When we read history, whether it be the history of Dives in the parable, or of Shylock in the play, we see how hard wealth can make men,— how it can contract their vision and dwarf their aspirations and extinguish their sympathies. Nay, when we read the lives of our fellowmen as they are lived alongside of us, we see how wealth can benumb the conscience and brutalize the moral sense, so that a rich man's career shall remind you of nothing so much as those buccaneers of the Spanish main with whom might made right, and who knew no law but the law of a triumphant audacity. When one notes these things, and sees what a power there is in the possession of wealth to stimulate the instincts of cruelty and a petty revenge, and to extinguish those finer traits which make life sweet and sunny—above all, when one sees how riches rear a dome of brass over so many human lives, and make heaven and Christ and the life that is to come as unlonged-for and unappreciated as would be a lock of a dead child's hair to a pawnbroker—then one can at least understand why Christ should say, "It is easier for a camel to go through the eye of a needle, than for a rich man to enter into the kingdom of God."

Yes, it may be answered, one can understand why Christ should say it, but one can not easily understand why any one else should think it worth while to repeat it just now—least of all why the pulpit should make of it a theme for these present hours. Five or ten years ago, when speculation was rife and values were inflated and half the world was mad with the craze of finding some short cut to easy fortune, men needed to be reminded that the greed of gain and a false estimate of the value of wealth were dangerous things. But in these hours of shrinking values and vanishing fortunes, of diminished incomes and straitened means, such cautions are, to say the least, a trifle superfluous. Experience, or if you choose, Providence, is teaching men that riches very easily take to themselves wings and fly away, and the question with a good many of us is not how we shall hold on to what we have, but how much longer some of us shall have any thing to hold on to. At such a time these scriptural cautions about the dangers of wealth have much the same appropriateness as a solemn admonition concerning intemperance to a man whose daily diet is bread and whose daily drink is water.

Such an answer, spoken or unspoken, shows how essentially superficial may easily be one's view of the whole matter. Who does not know that wealth is shrinking and incomes diminishing, and perplexity and uncertainty widely increasing? All that goes without saying, and no man could pretend to ignore it if he would. But the question which lies behind is the question. "How are people bearing this sort of ordeal? What is the temper that it evokes? What are the characters that it is educating? What is the tone of the times?

It is the way in which a man parts with a thing that shows best of all how he values it—how large a part of his life it has been—what he himself considers life to be without it, in one word how far identified the camel and his hump, the pack mule and his pannier, the man and his money, have come to be! I do not wonder that when in these times widows and orphans are stripped in a moment of their all, they should find it hard to submit, and harder still to accept the struggle and penury to which henceforth, through no fault of their own, they are doomed. As a matter of fact, however, these are the classes who, so far as I have encountered them, have, on the whole, accepted their reverses, with noblest fortitude and with most uncomplaining submission. How has it been with others? Is it not true that from those, who have themselves largely contributed to the present condition of things,—who have been more self-indulgent than vigilant, more rash than prudent, more prodigal than forecasting, more eager for gain than scrupulous as to methods of acquiring it, one hears a querulous, peevish, resentful, ungenerous tone which is simply contemptible. Even if one's belongings were a far more integral portion of his character and personality than they can possibly be, men ought to be ashamed to whimper and scold and complain as some men are doing nowadays, because they have been called to part with those belongings. But the worst of such a temper—a temper that in these days hardens itself against its fellowman, and resents an appeal to its sympathies as an ill-timed impertinence—is to be found in the fact that it is such a dismal revelation of the things that such men most prize and love,—that it shows to us with such startling and almost shocking distinctness that if you part the gentlemanly, well-bred, portly fellow-citizen and his money, there is no certainty that you may not find in him to-morrow a soured, embittered and resentful blasphemer. Is it any wonder that Christ spoke plain words to such a temper, and are not these even more than others the times in which to be reminded of them ?

Bear with me then, if in speaking this morning of the perils of wealth I use great plainness of speech. It ought at least to set us to thinking, if when we come to part with our money we find it so like the rending asunder of body and soul to let it go. It ought to set us to thinking if, when we anticipate misfortune, no misfortune seems to us so much to be dreaded as a catastrophe which threatens our property. This is the mammon-worship which, in the ultimate outcome of it, is the death of goodness, the death of nobleness, the death of aspiration. The kingdom of God, whether here or hereafter, must needs be made up of those in whose breasts a sentiment of personal loyalty to a personal Master is sovereign and supreme. If we do not love Christ well enough to part cheerfully with every thing else, if need be, so long as we are not parted from Him, then verily we are none of His. And if any of us have lately been disciplined by personal losses, by business disappointments, by straitened means, believe me, it has been because He would fain have us learn to love Him better than gold or silver, and to put His fellowship above the indulgence of our tastes or the gratification of our ambitions. To come to the gate of heaven when this little life is ended, with a shrivelled soul and a starved heart; to stand there looking back and feeling that we have left behind us in houses and lands, bonds and bank-stock, every thing that gave us consideration with our fellows and consequence before the world, this, it seems to me, is as dismal a vision as the imagination could call up. And this is the peril of the longing for, or possession of, wealth.

Let us thank God that He has made it possible to avoid such a peril. If history is thick-strewn with the examples of those in whom wealth has wrought moral insensibility and spiritual deadness; if it has taught us how rich a man may be, and as a consequence how selfish; if it has shown us how it can blind men's eyes and harden their hearts,—it has shown us, also, how

its possessor may accept it as a trust, and use it as a
stewardship, and ennoble it as an instrument of divinest service. Two men have passed away during
the past week—one in our own city, and another in
the city of Philadelphia—whose history, as one turns
from their graves to sum it up, is at once a poem and
a benediction. They were both men of large wealth
and of inherited culture. They were both men with
an intense love of life, and most human enjoyment
of its pleasures. No man who ever saw Theodore
Roosevelt in the saddle in the Park, or in his seat at
a dinner-table would have been guilty of the silly
impertinence of calling him a bloodless ascetic or a
dyspeptic saint. No man who ever met William Welsh,
in his house or on 'Change, would have said that he
did not know the meaning of pleasure or the delight
of acquisition. There have not lived in our generation
two men who were more thoroughly alive, to their
very finger ends, or who were more conspicuously
exposed to the manifold dangers of the possession
of great wealth. Of great wealth, I say, for they
were, both of them, men whose incomes dwarfed and
belittled the vast majority of those among whom they
lived and moved. And yet who, in thinking of them,
ever thought of their money? And when they died
the other day, bereaving the two chief cities of our
land with a sense of personal loss, who asked concerning either of them so beggarly a question as,

"What did he leave?" What did they leave? They left each one of them the fragrance of a good name, which is as ointment poured out. They left their image stamped in the hearts of thousands of men and women and children whose lives they had brightened and ennobled and blessed. Above all, they left a lesson to you and me of what men can be and do who say to wealth and the world, "You are my servant, not my master! I will be not slothful in business; I will be fervent in spirit, but it shall be always 'serving the Lord.'" They have taught two great communities that it is possible to be rich and not selfish, to have wealth and not be enslaved by it, to use the world as not abusing it. And to-day, William Weish, in the Indian wigwam in Niobrara, among the boys of Girard College with whom he spent a part of every Sunday of his life, in the homes of the working men of Frankford whom he taught to love him as a brother man;—and Theodore Roosevelt in the newsboy's lodging house, in the cripples' hospital, in the heart of the little Italian flower-girl who brought her offering of grateful love to his door the day he died, have left behind them monuments the like of which mere wealth could never rear, and the proudest achievements of human genius never hope to win. They will be remembered when the men of great fortune who have filled the brief hour with the fame of their millions shall have vanished into merited oblivion. They may have been poorer than these, but the world is richer because they were in it, and the influence of their large-hearted and unselfish lives will be owned and honored when the mere hoarders of the day have ceased to have any slightest interest or influence among men, save as subjects of the somewhat curious and somewhat contemptuous study of the moral anatomist.

See then, whether you have wealth or merely covet it, the lesson of such lives to you and me. Wealth is dangerous, and the worshipper of mammon, whether he dwell in a palace or a hovel, will find it equally hard to find an entrance into the kingdom of God. But wealth, like other dangerous powers, may be subjected to a wise discipline and a resolute control. Lightning is dangerous, but men have mastered it and made it do their bidding. Master your meaner lust for gain and then make it do your bidding in the service of your heavenly Master. It is not how many bonds you have in a bank vault, or how much plate on your side-board that God looks to see, but how many lives have been brightened and how many sorrows have been healed by the gifts of your love. The cause of Christ, the cause of truth, the cause of humanity need your gifts. But none of them need them half so much as you need the blessed and ennobling education of being permitted to give them.

And therefore let us ask God, in the spirit of One who, though He was rich became poor that we through His poverty might be made rich, that He would teach us whether we have much or little, to bring ourselves and our belongings, and with equal and entire devotion surrender both to Him.

SERMON VII.

THE SLAUGHTER OF THE INNOCENTS.

ST. MATTHEW II. 16.

" Then Herod . . . was exceeding wroth, and sent forth and slew all the children that were in Bethlehem, and in all the coasts thereof, from two years old and under." *

THE number of these children, however, was not great. The population of Bethlehem and its suburbs (which is what is meant by the phrase "all the coasts thereof") was about two thousand souls, and it is not probable therefore that the number of children under two years old, was more than twenty-five or thirty. Many times that number die in New York from common or epidemic diseases every week, and nobody hears any thing about it.

And yet, the prominence which this slaughter of the innocents holds in New Testament history is not exaggerated nor unintentional. As little unintelligible or inappropriate is the equal prominence which the Church gives to the memory of those little chil-

---

* New York, Holy Innocents' Day, Dec. 28, 1879.

dren in the services of this Holy Innocents' Day. They were not martyrs, and save as they were untainted by contact with actual sin, they were not " Holy." But there is something in the thought that Christ is no sooner born than human malice begins to hate and strike at Him, which makes it impossible not to regard with exceptional interest those who were the victims of that malice. And then, there is something appalling in the power of a cruel nature to assail and kill out a young and unoffending life, which makes the death of these twenty or thirty little children at least worthy of being remembered.

For, after all, both they and their murderer are types. The Herods are not all dead nor are the murdered innocents all buried. We think of Herod as a person who, for the credit of the race be it said, was horribly exceptional in his cruelty. And in a sense, this is true. It has been brought to light as evidence of the pre-eminent brutality of the man, that near the close of his reign he gave orders for the execution of many of the leading men of Judea, providing that they should be put to death immediately before he died himself. In this way, he said, he would be sure of at least some genuine mourning in connection with his own funeral. It was this same Herod too who put to death two of the sons of his wife Mariamne, and later, his own son, Antipater, and it was of him that the Emperor Augustus observed, that "it was better to be Herod's swine than Herod's son." Add to this that he was the ruler of a con-quered people—that he lived in an era of imperial absolutism (*"imperium sed non libertas,"*) and that he was himself a man of violent and ungoverned passions; and his whole proceeding becomes equally probable and intelligible. There had been born in Bethlehem one whom astrologers and magi from the East were seeking, as the future King of the Jews. There must be no rival near the throne, protested equally the ambition and the selfishness of Herod. And what seemed easier, as a way of removing that rival before he grew old enough to be dangerous, than to slaughter him and every other infant in the neighborhood where he had been born? And thus selfishness and greed—the greed of power, of place, of self-will—have their way, and helpless innocency is slaughtered.

Has it ceased, even yet, to be sacrificed to the same cruel and deadly instincts? We have no longer ny Herods in high places, and the old despotisms with their arbitrary decrees of life and death, have almost ceased to have even a name to live,—at least in the civilized world. We come back to this blessed Christmas-tide thankful almost more than for any thing else, that God has taught us, by His Son's birth into our childhood, how sacred and holy all childhood was meant to be. We look upon our

children as hallowed and consecrated by His infancy and boyhood who was once a babe, a child,
as they are. But can it be said that the world—
our world—has altogether purged itself of the guilt
of the murder of its innocents? At the first view
nothing can be more inspiring than the contrast
between the civilization of our time and that of the
world when Christ entered it. Think of the condition of childhood then and now. Consider what
art and science and philanthropy have done to
widen the horizon of a child's education, to guard
and invigorate his health, to protect him from the
brutality of ignorant or heartless parenthood. A
book might be written about the beneficent schemes
which have been originated and set on foot in our
own generation alone for the exclusive benefit of
children.

But you can not have the benefits of a high civilization without its penalties. You can not have the
crowded life, the eager competitions, the manifold in-
timacies of a great city without their perils. The
factory loom means the factory hand. The cheapened product means the cheapened producer. Now
then, go and stand at the mouth of an English coal
mine. I do not speak of English factories, because
a wise legislation has largely reformed the wrongs
that were formerly done in them to undergrown and
overworked children. But see the boys and girls that

emerge, when the day is done, from the mouth of a
Welsh coal pit. It is enough to make the heart ache
to note the wan, pale faces of these little ones who
have never seen a ray of sunshine all day long. But,
"thank God!" we say, "we have nothing like that in
America." No, not just like it perhaps, but in great
seven-storied buildings in this New York of ours
there are other children at work in an atmosphere
even more unwholesome, and at tasks which are far
more hurtful. It would be a very instructive experience for any one who will seek it, to walk down
this very thoroughfare or those in its immediate
neighborhood, about six o'clock in the evening in the
early springtime say, and see the half-grown throngs
that emerge from our various manufactories. It may
be that there is no real cruelty in any individual instance, but the thing that is most of all depressing
is, that the higher we lift the scale of our civilization,
the fiercer seems to be the struggle which some
classes among us have to make in order to live at
all, and the harder press the burdens of life upon
those whose puny shoulders are least able to bear
them.

II. But it is undoubtedly true that the conscience
of most communities is by no means insensible to
these physical cruelties to children, nor slow to rebuke and discourage them. How is it when we as-

cend a step higher, and turn from the body to the mind? We Americans have an enormous pride in our system of popular education, and the first thing that a foreigner is taken to see when he comes among us, is a public school. It is a spectacle which will abundantly reward any one who will take the trouble to see it. The service which our common schools have rendered in placing the ordinary advantages of education within the reach of multitudes who would otherwise have been without them, is simply incalculable. But they have nevertheless produced two results which are equally harmful and deteriorating. They have largely lifted off the sense of parental responsibility in the training of the mind, and they have made the education of children in large masses a mechanical rather than a rational process. One of the hardest things in the world to do is to think. There are multitudes of people who receive impressions, and echo them, and who mistake such a process for thinking; but we have only to consider how rare is the power of clear statement about any but the very simplest thing to realize how little most people think. The one infallible test of understanding any thing is the being able to put your understanding of it into such clear and consecutive statement that another shall be able to understand it.

But in order that one shall learn to do this, two things are necessary: one is, that we shall learn what-

ever we set about to learn, otherwise than by mere
rote; and the other is, that our teacher shall have been
able to kindle in us what Lord Bacon has most felicitously called the "enthusiasm of knowledge." Have
you never known what it was to have another's clear
insight and strong personality take a subject otherwise dull and dry, and so inform and infuse it with
life that the cold and formal science became a glowing and vital organism, as different from what it had
seemed to you in the pages of a book as is the liquid
and incandescent lava flinging its meteoric splendors
from the mouth of Vesuvius, from the dead and col-
orless ashes and scoriæ that lie extinct about its
foot! It is thus that that godlike thing, the reason,
was meant to throb and glow. Is it a small matter
that, in so many men and women, the world over,
the intellect has never been kindled to enthusiasm,
and has long ago fallen into the rut of a mechanical
perfunctoriness? Has it never occurred to us to wonder what we shall one day be doing, in another world,
and how, not the hand, but the mind will busy itself,
when that life shall have been entered upon, in which
there will be no more tasks for the hand, but only
for the mind and the heart? "Flesh and blood," says
the apostle, "can not inherit the kingdom of God."
Then, in that kingdom, there will be no raiment to
weave and fashion and adorn. We shall be done forever with the question of dress-patterns and orna-

ments and jewellery. The problem over which it may be we have spent hours, as to what shade of color to wear with what other shade, will be of infinitely less consequence than the height of the great wall of China. We shall not be building houses nor furnishing them any more; for, again, if we are to believe the apostle, we shall have "a house not made with hands, eternal in the heavens." But, when we get to that house, what are we going to do? We keep our hands and feet and eyes busy now, just as we feed husks into a threshing-machine to prevent it from wearing upon itself. But we shall have left the husks all behind us then, and if we have never learned to think, in the face of all the magnificent problems which wait for their solution in that other life, what are we going to do with our minds? O father, who art sending your boy to college and giving your children the costliest masters that the town affords,— whose whole intercourse with those of whose being, under God, you are the author, is a brief salutation at the breakfast or dinner table and a hurried caress as you hasten away to your business,—consider that your child may be stuffed with words like a parrot, and all the while never have learned to use the mind which distinguishes him from the parrot as an immortal being. There is an education which trains the legs and the hands and the tongue, and which yet stifles or starves the reason. And that may be the slaughter of the innocents, though all the while it is carried on with utmost cost and care.

III. But there is a worse and deadlier murder still. God is forever teaching us that, godlike as is the reason, there is something in man that is diviner even than reason. There have been great teachers and statesmen and commanders, who have moved the world by their intellects; but the Being who has most deeply moved it, though He included within Himself all imaginable possibilities of intellectual supremacy, has left the most lasting impress upon the race, not so much because of the sovereignty of His intellect as of His affections. It has been by His goodness, rather than by His knowledge, that Christ has conquered and won the hearts of men. And that, in children, which in spite of inherited infirmities and original sin, most touches and attracts us is their childish innocence, their instinctive recoil from what is wrong, their sensitiveness to reproof or disapprobation. What is the world of to-day doing—nay, what are we doing—to guard and protect this highest life? There was a murder of the innocents, and there is a murder of innocence; and, as God is our judge, we shall find that the latter is a darker and wickeder deed than the former. "Keep innocency and do the thing that is right," says the Psalmist, "for that shall bring a man peace at the last." But how can our children "keep innocency" when the manners, and the talk, and the example, and the reading of their elders so often and so cruelly conspire against it?

In addressing a company of teachers, I think, at Birmingham the other day, Mr. John Bright spoke of the discouragements with which they had to contend whose calling it was to impress or reform adults. "Men and women" (he said in substance), "hear sermons and appeals and addresses, and are too often astonishingly little affected by them; but the man or woman whose office is that of a teacher of children ministers to a congregation who, if his heart is in his work, will respond to his slightest touch." We may lead them as we will. We may mould these young natures by our most unconscious pressure. And the appalling fact is that we do. The eager eyes that watch us all the while so closely, take in the meaning of a thousand things that we do, whose meaning we ourselves are never thinking of. The seeming truth that was, and was meant to be, half a lie,—they detect it, though the guest in your drawing-room to whom it was uttered may not. The books which we are willing to read ourselves, though we sternly prohibit them to them, they will learn to thirst for a knowledge of by a law as old as the curiosity of our first mother. And our prayer-less lives, our uncharitable speech, our poor and sordid ambitions, ah! they are learning these things with a facility which we do not even dream of.

And when they pass out of our immediate companionship, what is it that awaits them beyond? The old-fashioned doctrine of the deep and utter depravity of human nature is in our day widely challenged; and yet there are devices for the murder of the innocents in our age and in this community, beside which the slaughter of Herod was an act of paternal benignity. There are some things, of which the apostle declares it is a shame even to speak, and it is doubtful whether the pulpit is ever more gravely misused than when, under the pretence of rebuking them, particular sins and shames are made the topic of a sermon. But there are wrongs that exist among us, and of which all men know; there are crimes against good morals in which art and the press and the public mails have all alike been employed, and for which men, sentenced to state-prison for their commission, have been pardoned by those high in authority, which ought to rouse every man among us with one single spark of manhood in him to lash their infamous authors and abettors with the scourge of a swift and fiery indignation. In the early days of Christianity they flung young girls to wild beasts in the amphitheatre. To-day, with a more deliberate and more devilish ingenuity, men line life with pitfalls for the innocent feet of childhood, and earn vast fortunes by destroying the souls of our little ones. Let us see to it that neither you nor I, by our carelessness, our indifference, our heartlessness, become aiders and abettors in the same crime.

There is not one of us here to-day, I am persuaded, who does not think sometimes regretfully and tenderly of his own childhood. As you look at your children amid these Christmas-tide festivities, does it not sometimes occur to you to envy the simple and innocent pleasure which they have in simple and innocent things? How the little faces glow with a surprised delight which you feel can never be yours again! There is sadness in the thought, and in the fact there is danger as well. There is such a thing as becoming cold-hearted as we grow older, and of ceasing to care very greatly about any thing. We have had our disappointments, it may be. The venture of love that we made exhales to-day the perfume of myrrh rather than of rose-leaves. There has been not a little bitterness in our cup, and perhaps some great grief has left us with that stunned and benumbed feeling from which the heart is so slow to recover. But what is it then that melts and softens us when nothing else will? "And Jesus took a little child and set him in the midst of them!" It was the hardness of unbrotherly ambition and human selfishness that Christ thus softened. But not less potent is the child to melt that other hardness, born not of our selfishness, but of our griefs and our disappointments. And therefore, let us turn to these little ones and ask that they may soften and rejuvenate us, while we guard and shelter them. Be not too eager to dismiss them to the care of nursery-maids and preceptors. They want the nurture of your unselfish love far more than they want any other nurture. The son of a man very eminent in one of the learned professions in England, was once standing in a felon's dock, awaiting a sentence of transportation. Said the judge, who knew his parentage and his history, "Do you remember your father?" "Perfectly," said the youth; "whenever I entered his presence he said, 'Run away, my lad, and don't trouble me.'" The great lawyer was thus enabled to complete his famous work on the law of trusts, and his son, in due time, furnished a practical commentary on the way in which his father had discharged that most sacred of all trusts committed to him in the person of his own child.

Not all of us here are fathers or mothers. But, in a sense, we are all of us the guardians of weakness, of innocence, and so of childhood. At some point or other in the great circle of our social life we may bring to bear our influence in the interest of little children. By our love, by our sympathy, by our patient (ah! how much patience it often needs), by our patient, painstaking, personal interest we can guard the innocents from a death ten thousand times more dreary and hopeless than theirs who perished in Bethlehem. This is Hospital Sunday, and to-day you will be asked for your offerings for those who are housed, by the charity of their more favored brethren, in these hotels of God. Some of you have seen the children's ward at St. Luke's or a child's hospital elsewhere. Is there on earth a more pathetic sight? These helpless little ones, crippled, deformed, emaciated, yet often with such infinite patience and sweetness on their faces. Blessed be God, you say, for the Christian benevolence which has done so much to ease their pain, and soften their penury, and heal their diseases! Blessed be God for His gentle and loving servants, that have dedicated themselves unreservedly to a ministry among these shattered and helpless sufferers! And yet, as we watch the cripple in his wheeled chair, or the little hunch-back bolstered up in bed, we can not but think of other homes where fair and shapely children are bounding to and fro, and where no disfigurement or deformity has ever come. Would to God that we could make those little cripples and sufferers and invalids as straight and strong and as ruddy as they! It is well to ease the pain and soften the bitterness of deformity as we may; but oh! if only we could have guarded these childish victims from the cruelty, the neglect, the maltreatment which made them what they are!

Even so of those other deformities not of the body,

but of the soul.   God can forgive the sinner and wash the vilest soul in the blood of His dear Son.   But how much better for us, and for our little ones, to be kept pure and stainless by His Spirit, until, at last, redeemed from all sin and uncleanness, we and they shall be presented "spotless before the presence of His glory!"

SERMON VIII.

PEARLS BEFORE SWINE.

ST. MATTHEW VII. 6.

" Give not that which is holy unto the dogs, neither cast ye your pearls before swine, lest they trample them under their feet, and turn again and rend you." *

THE dogs, here, are men, and so are the swine. In other words, Christ gives us, in this verse, a rule to govern us in our intercourse with our fellows, not in our dealing with brutes. "It goes without saying" that to take, for instance, the sacramental bread from yonder altar and to give it to the dogs, would be a most indecent sacrilege; and equally and obviously it is true, that to cast pearls before swine for the purpose, let us say, of discovering whether the swine can discriminate between pearls and acorns, would be utter and outrageous folly. We do not need that Christ should tell us that, and it is in fact something else and of infinitely graver import that He does tell us. Just before, He had been saying, "Judge not." Do not be too eager to spy out the faults of other people. And then there comes that crisp and com-

---

* New York, November 19, 1876.

pact statement of the truth He was trying to lodge in the minds of His listeners which He utters in the brief parable of the mote and the beam. There are plenty of people with motes in their eyes, but before you undertake to pull them out look after the beam in your own. In other words, do not cultivate a vision too microscopic, too critical—"judge not." But straightway He goes on to say, "though you are not to judge, you are not to be blind. You are to recognize a dog when you see it, and the swine when you see them, and to act accordingly. Keep holy things for holy handling. Cast not your pearls before swine."

I wonder that criticism, ready as it is to make issue with the words of Christ, has never objected to these words that "they are uncharitable." Is it not hard measure to call a man a dog, and to describe a whole class of people as swine? For here, as I began by saying, Christ is talking about men and women, and not about brutes at all. And in calling some people "dogs" and others "swine" is there not an absence of that tenderness and charity which we are wont to look for in the speech of Christ? Possibly; but then I do not know that we have any warrant for assuming that Christ's words were always to be tuned to the key of tenderness. Truth must sometimes be very rugged and out-spoken and abrupt. Above all it must by its very nature, be true; it must call a spade a spade,

and Christ by virtue also of His nature must give
to dog-like and swinish dispositions their own name,
and speak of them as they are. Such people are
in the world, and it is wisdom, not harshness, to
rate them as they deserve, and to bear ourselves
accordingly. We are not indeed to judge, but a
dog is to be accounted a dog, and swine are to be
estimated as swine.

It is high time, I venture to think, that we lifted
this truth to the level of a rightful and regnant authority. Is it said that there is a good deal of uncharitableness in the world—a great deal of harsh
judgment, and bitter speech, and ungenerous innuendo? Yes, verily, and we shall do well to deplore
it, and better still to try and mend it. But over
against this habitual tartness of criticism there is
(one is sometimes tempted to think) an habitual
laxness of judgment which is the worse evil of the
two. Every body, we seem many of us to think, is
rather selfish and rather faulty and rather insincere,
but nobody is a dog or a swine, or at any rate we
can not think of acting towards them as though
they were. There is something due to good breed-
ing, and if society includes certain people, certain
customs, and a certain literature, one can not be
expected to make issue with the circumstances in
which he finds himself. I shall not stop now to inquire whether this sort of reasoning is true or false, nor

8

to ask (what would be, as I think you will acknowl-edge, a much more pertinent question) whether it is Christian or courageous. For after all, the issue which it raises is one which in this discussion is altogether wide of the mark. The question started by these words of Christ's is not as to what we will say or do, but rather as to what we will refrain from saying or doing. It is a question, in other words, not of action, but simply of reserve. There are some things, says the Master, which in some companies you may wisely keep back. There are pearls which ought not to be cast before swine. Guard your pearls, lest they before whom you strew them trample them under foot and turn and rend you !

I. And one of them is the pearl of innocence. I know that a certain school of theology tells us that that is a lost pearl, and one which humanity forfeited in the beginning. Very well, we need have no dis-pute with such. The evil possibilities of human na-ture are very great and very dark. When Hazael says to the prophet, "Is thy servant a dog that he should do this thing," and then ultimately goes and does it, he shows us that the blackest depravity may develop itself out of what seems the fairest soil of guilelessness. But all this does not prevent one mak-ing a distinction between experience and inexperi-ence, familiarity and unfamiliarity in sin, concerning which the most pertinent thing just here to recognize is that it is a perfectly true and valid distinction. There is such a thing as innocence that may be smirched, and guilelessness that may be corrupted, and pearls of purity that may be cast before swine. There is a blessed ignorance of much that happens in this "miserable and naughty world," which is itself a treasure above price, and there is oftentimes a simple-hearted and unsuspecting disclosure of that ignorance which swinish natures, by virtue of the coarse instincts that govern them, delight to drag down into the mire and cover all over with the filth and ooze of a guilty knowledge. And here it is therefore that this precept of Christ finds its foremost, if not its most urgent, application. I speak to a great many here this morning who are still in the first freshness of their days, and to whom God has given what David calls in phrase of such matchless fitness, "the dew of their youth." Believe me, fellow-pilgrims and soldiers, the hot sun will rise soon enough and burn away those dews. There is an inevitable contact with the evil of life which will make you bitterly familiar, before you have done with it, with all of that evil which you will need to know. But meantime, there is a great deal more of it that you have no need to know—there is a great deal more which you will be immeasurably better and happier for never knowing, and which your Master, in these words of the text, tells you how to avoid knowing. There are those about you who find delight in such things. There is a "set" in most societies, and at any rate there are individuals in every community whose function seems to be to root among unclean things. If you are a young man and are willing to parade your ignorance before them, they will turn it into loathsome knowledge fast enough. If you are a young girl and are willing to listen to some women, they will brush the bloom off the tender fruit with a hand as ruthless as it is expert. There are companies and companionships where no indecorous word will be spoken perhaps, but where by the language of equivocation and by an artful play upon words enough is conveyed to dye the cheek of any right-minded and sensitive listener with honest and indignant blushes. And in such companies and before such listeners it is that the disclosure of one's innocence is simply casting pearls before swine. What care such persons that they are staining a sweet and unspotted nature with all hideous and defiling images? They like to startle, to shock, to surprise. The most odious thing is, to them as to the swine, the most welcome. And if you will cast down your innocence before them, they will trample it under foot, and then if they have degraded you enough for their own guilty ends, they will turn again and rend you.

And, therefore, refuse to listen to such persons.

Refuse to disclose to them your own blessed ignorance. Refuse, by any artifice of theirs, to be piqued
into that curiosity which they are thirsting so basely
to gratify. Guard the pearl of your own innocence!

And guard it, too, from swinish books as well as
from swinish people. Eighty per cent, eighty volumes out of every one hundred, eight hundred out of
the thousand volumes that are taken out of our cir-
culating libraries every day are, we have just been
told, works of fiction, and there are some young persons who read two novels a day. How many of
them, do you suppose, are fit to read? How many
of them, think you, leave a clean taste behind them
when one lays them down? How many of them,
will any of us undertake to say, are not full of the
treatment of diseased and evil emotions? And when
it comes to French, and even German fiction sometimes, how much worse it is. We talk about the
corruption of letters in the time of Martial and Petro-
nius, but he was right who lately affirmed, on the
other side of the Atlantic, that "no literature of fiction or drama has ever sunk into such a pit of filth
as modern French light literature." Certainly "no
literature has ever so lowered the standard of culture
and morality and innocence; no literature has ever
so thrown overboard honor and truth in order to
revel in vice; no literature has ever so stained all
the ideals most sacred to God-fearing and man-lov-

ing men, nor heaped ridicule so basely upon all that is pure and homely and simple and lovely, as this branch of the literature of France." And therefore whether it be French in tongue or simply in tone, be afraid of such literature. If you ever find yourself, when reading a book, glad that you are alone, and relieved that no friend whose good opinion you respect is looking over your shoulder, take that book with a pair of tongs and make of it straightway a burnt-offering at the shrine of common decency. Do not fling down your innocence to be trampled upon by any brutal vulgarity in a book, any more than by any brutal vulgarity incarnate in men or women. Remember that that pearl of guileless unfamiliarity with evil once dropped into the mire, can never be regained, and that there are those all about you whose daily and nightly cross it is that once long ago they so foolishly, uselessly and wantonly flung theirs away!

II. And so too of the pearl of reverence: "Give not that which is holy unto the dogs," says Christ, and so reminds us of that universal recognition of the difference between things holy and unholy which is one of the primal instincts of the human soul. And this, my brother, is the signature of your origin. No theory of the substantial identity of your own nature with that of those ranks of creation which are below you has been able, in the smallest degree, to account for the human instincts of worship and reverence. It is an instinct which has distinguished no order of the brute creation, however high. It is an instinct which is wanting in no order of the human race however low. A chimpanzee is so horribly like some people whom we all know that when I have looked at one I have been readier than after whole volumes of argument to say, "I strike my flag. There is no essential difference between a man and a monkey, after all." But, there is this difference. No monkey ever built an altar. No chimpanzee ever framed a language and formulated it into a prayer. No faintest sign of reverence for any unseen power ever bent the knees of an ape. You and I are allied to the divine by this invariable instinct of reverence. It prompts us to faith in the invisible, to acts of worship and honor before our Maker, to obedience to our own conscience. But it is an instinct against which there is a great deal in our time which seems to be conspiring. I am not referring now to the tendency of scientific inquiry which, whatever may be its temper, can only have one blessed and helpful tendency and one bright and sure result, but I have in mind that widely-diffused sentiment of indifference and derision concerning sacred things and sacred instincts which I deplore not so much in the interests of Him whom it dishonors as of those whom it deteriorates.

Is it an uncommon thing to hear sacred themes, the holiest aspirations, the loftiest interests treated with a light and rather cynical levity? Is there no young person within the sound of my voice this morning who has been drawn out by some cleverly veiled questioner, only to be met with the patronizing protest, "But really now, you can not pretend that you believe in" this, or that, or the other thing, which, it may be, is something which ought to be as dear as life itself? Are there none among us who know what it is to be drawn into discussions where every unsuspecting admission is made a pitfall to entrap the unwary feet, and where the whole aim seems to be to shake one loose from the very foundations of the faith? Nay, worse still, are there none of us who have encountered that saddest faithlessness of all, which treats nothing as sacred or true or worthy of reverence—which finds only hollowness and falsehood in all divinest things, and which owns no goodness or virtue or faith as existing anywhere?

Now then, observe, I do not say that we are to stifle all questionings and ignore our deepest perplexities. On the contrary, I would fain have you feel that you are not to be afraid of them—that we are to own them, and not needlessly to condemn ourselves because of them; and above all, that we are courageously to grapple with them. But that is one thing. It is quite another thing to spread out our deepest feelings to be the languid amusement of any chance lounger who may have nothing better to do than to make sport of them. Holy things demand holy handling. But any one who will only turn over your faith in your unseen Lord with, as it were, the coarse curiosity of a swine's snout, had better be kept aloof from it. With such persons the wise and wholesome course is simple reserve. Give not that which is holy unto the dogs, neither cast the pearl of your godward reverence before swine.

III. And so, finally, of that other pearl most priceless, and yet I think the oftenest squandered, the pearl of our affections. O, the wrongs that have been perpetrated in the sacred name of friendship, and under the shield of the sanctity of love ! What confidences have been betrayed, what pledges have been broken, what miseries have been entailed upon those whose only fault has been that they have flung down at another's feet the pearl of an utter trust and an all-absorbing affection ! Such a trust and such an affection are among the most precious possibilities of youth; and who shall say how often youth has given them both, only to find that they have been casting pearls before swine. There are men who delight to gain the confidence and win the devotion of other men who are younger than themselves, and then use the mastery which they have won to degrade the young natures that have given it. There are those to whom the freshness and guilelessness of early manhood are a perpetual reproach, and who meet that chivalrous deference which it is the first instinct of a high-spirited youth to pay to age by striving, first, to secure the attachment of such a youth, and then, if they can, to make him twofold more the child of hell than themselves. And therefore to any one of us who is as yet upon the threshold of life, there is no warning so pre-eminently pertinent as that which bids him guard the treasure of his affections. There are those, thank God, who are equally worthy of our trust and our love; but if, for any reason, our walk in life seems to lead us apart from these, then it is better,—aye, a thousand times better,—that we should go on from the beginning all the way on to the end solitary and alone. I know how dreary and forbidding such counsel may sound, but what shall we say of that which is too often its alternative? I know that there are many of us to whom it seems most of all clear that their happiness in life, if they are to find it at all, is to be found in the outgoing of a great and absorbing affection. But do you need that I should rehearse to you the history of those who, hurried away by some impulse of restlessness and unreflection, have flung down their all at the feet of those who were no better than the dogs and the swine? Need I rehearse to you the history of others who, seeing the pearl of a heart's purest devotion thus trampled under foot, have known, too, what it was to have the brutal nature turn and rend them in its cruel greed because they were not the coarse thing that it would fain have had them? Is there any thing more bitterly patent, when we look over the face of our modern life, than that a large part of the misery of human existence comes from the all but wanton recklessness with which one sex flings down the treasure of its love to be too often spurned and trampled upon by the other? And therefore, O young and trusting heart, guard the pearl of your innocence; guard the pearl of your reverence; but most of all, guard the pearl of your affections!

And that we may, let us learn early to bring them to the feet of One whose infinite heart of tenderness and love will prize them most of all. Nay, whether it be early or late in our day, let us bring our deepest reverence and our best affections to our Lord, and then, if we have lost the pearl of our innocence He will help us on the way toward that other and purer life where we may hope to seek and to find it again. Yes, He who knew what it was to discover the pearls lost and buried in the mire, and to lift them back to the light again,—He who knew what it was to have very near to Him those who had flung away their guilelessness, their affections, and even their every hope,—He who knew how to succor and to save all

these will do no less for us. Let us try to understand how safe our best treasures will be in His
keeping, and then let us ask Him to show Himself to every better instinct in us, whether it be of
purity, of reverence, or of love. Come forth, O thou
Christ of Mary and of Martha, of worldly Matthew
and of tempted Peter—come forth out of the cloud
and shadow and show us thy perfect self! Fill us
with a divine discernment and discrimination, teach
us to abhor that which is evil and to cleave to that
which is good. Teach us to prize the pearls of innocence, of reverence, and of love; and that no swinish
feet may trample them in the mire, teach us to bring
them and lay them early at thine own.

SERMON IX.

THE DUTY OF WOMAN TO WOMEN.

JUDGES IV. 4, 14.

"And Deborah, a prophetess, the wife of Lapidoth, she judged Israel at that time. . . . . . And Deborah said unto Barak, Up, for this is the day in which the Lord hath delivered Sisera into thine hand." *

WE are here introduced to a woman with "a mission," as we say nowadays, and therefore not a woman likely to be interesting to the majority of those to whom I speak this evening. For it is a suggestive and on the whole perhaps a creditable fact that heroic women are not so interesting to women as to men. We read about that German prophetess who roused her people against the invaders from Rome, or about Joan of Arc, who, simple peasant girl that she was, communing with mysterious angels' voices (as the legend runs), kindled the French nation against the English dominion when princes and statesmen had well-nigh given up the cause; or we read about Deborah, like St. Louis under the oak at Vincennes, sitting under a Judean

---

* Packer Institute, Brooklyn, N. Y., June 13, 1877,

palm, not with downcast eyes and folded hands and extinguished hopes, but all on fire with faith and energy, with the soul of courage and the voice of command, and we are constrained to pay homage to her daring and her fearlessness, to her strong will and her unshrinking purpose. But if I were to ask any one of these young girls to whom I speak this evening whether she were ambitious of such a career, there is not one of you in a score who would say so. Women are not indifferent to admiration any more than men—in fact, they usually bear it with more equanimity—but a woman's idea of a happy and useful life is not usually a life of active effort on the platform or in public. A woman's idea of happiness and usefulness ordinarily centres (and who shall say that it does not rightly centre ?) in a home. First of all to have a home, and then to make it fair and bright, and then, if it may be, to share it with another to whom it shall be a welcome haven of rest and sunshine,—such a longing, which is simply the outcome of that divine instinct in accordance with which God long ago set the solitary in families, is surely as right as it is natural.

> "An ear that waits to catch
> A hand upon the latch,
>   A step that hastens its sweet rest to win;
> A world of care without,
> A world of strife shut out,
>   A world of love shut in."

"Such a vision dwells more or less in every woman's mind, except where poverty and misery have blotted it out. A poor woman, before a magistrate, being asked why she and her family, one of whom had died of hunger, did not take refuge in the alms-house, replied, 'We did not like to leave our home and our bits of comforts.'"*

Surely, we can not but revere this impulse, and all the more when we consider for how much the home stands. Nay, more, it is not wonderful, in view of these facts, that when any woman or set of women, undertakes to break out of the restraints of home, to proclaim a larger liberty for her sex, or demand what are called "Woman's rights," there should be on the part of the vast majority of that sex a decided disapproval of their course. Such persons are called "unwomanly,"—and sometimes they are, and women are wisely reminded that their proper sphere and their worthiest throne is in the home. All of which is true enough, and often timely enough.

But is there not something to be said on the other side, and is it not time that it was said? The young ladies of the Packer Institute to whom I am called to speak this evening have, I presume, most of them come here from homes each one of which is to each heart that turns to it to-night, the brightest spot in

---

* "Woman's Work and Woman's Culture," Intro. xxix. xxx.

all the world. To such homes you are looking forward to return, and in such homes or others like them it is your hope that your future may be passed. I pray God that it may be so; and I could ask no better boon for each one of you than that it shall be. But what are the probabilities that it will be so? What are the probabilities that the necessitudes of life may not break up these homes and leave more than one among us sooner or later without them? What is the certainty that any such thing as a home may be a possibility, I will not say to you who are here, but to multitudes of your sisters who are growing up in our day and in this land? We have been accustomed to hear the constantly reiterated assertion that "woman's sphere is the home." I confess for one that in view of the actual facts of society, as they exist around us, there is often in such words a sound of cruel irony. Do not you and I know, that there are thousands of women to whom a home is as impossible a thing as a castle in Spain? Do we not know that there are thousands of young girls in these two sister cities of ours who have no human being but themselves to depend upon, and who must somehow make their way and earn their own bread in life? Will you tell me how a home or anything else than a room and a hard, stern struggle for life is possible to these? Doubtless some of them will marry and preside over households of their own, but even if the marriage relation were the one invariable, inevitable, infallibly blessed relation for women which some people account it, what do you propose to do when already on the eastern coast of this new country of ours we have reached that condition which Mr. Greg, in his social judgments, refers to under the interrogative title, "Why are women redundant?" In other words, what shall we do with our superfluous women? There are eighty thousand more women than men in the state of Massachusetts alone. Now then, unless these eighty thousand are all women of fortune, it is a solemn trifling with a very grave and a very urgent problem to tell them that "woman's sphere is the home." A home implies a decent maintenance, a head who shall be its bread-winner, a common shelter and common belongings. It is Pharaoh commanding the captive Israelites to make brick without straw to bid the great army of solitary and dependent women back to the home, and when to this sort of exhortation there is added the sneer of ridicule or contempt for strong-minded women and women's rights and the like, it is adding mockery to heartlessness. Surely a woman has some rights as well as a man. Surely, too, among these is the right to earn her own living, and to maintain her own virtuous independence if there be none other to maintain her in virtuous dependence. And most surely of all, in every such endeavor

women deserve the most cordial sympathy of the
more favored of their own sex, and not less the generous approval of men. I presume I need not say
that I have no sympathy with any radicalism of female reform more than with any other extravagance,
but I confess I have felt with an Englishwoman who
said not long ago, "I wish it were felt that women
who are laboring for women are not necessarily one-
sided or selfish or self-asserting. . . . . When
men nobly born and possessing advantages of wealth
and education have fought the battles of poor men,
and have claimed and wrung from parliaments an
extension of privileges enjoyed by a few to classes
of their fellowmen who were toiling and suffering, I
do not remember ever to have heard them charged
with self-seeking; on the contrary, the regard that
such men have had for the rights of their fellowmen
has been praised, and deservedly so, as noble and
unselfish." And the same writer goes on to ask, in
substance, why it is that the endeavors of men for
men cease to be praiseworthy when they become the
endeavors of women for women?

For we have now reached a point in the social
progress of this age when it is necessary that we
should every one of us recognize the crisis that is
upon us. It is a transition-period from the old state
of labor for men and domesticity for women, to a
period in which there must be found labor for women

as well as for men. A much larger number of women must hereafter support themselves than have ever done so before. When some have married, and others have devoted themselves to education, and others to domestic service (you have all read I presume about the lady helps who are being introduced into English households in order that women of culture and refinement may have a decent maintenance and shelter over their heads), there still remain large numbers of women who are utterly unprovided for. How shall they be provided for? The East, as you know, has answered that question by the institution of polygamy which provides a nominal protection to a number of women most of whom are in fact simply servants of various grades and duties. The West has provided for it, at any rate in the Roman Communion, as in France and elsewhere, by the convent. Mr. Bloomfield, in his interesting work on Brittany, states that "the reason which oftentimes fills the convents of that country is poverty, not religion. A man has a large family of daughters; what is he to do with them? Marriage is less easy in France than in England, *i. e.*, marriage without fortune." A woman must have her *dot*, and the commercial negotiation in connection with a French marriage is often the most serious part of the whole affair. But what if there is no dowry to settle —no *dot* to transfer? Something must be done. "The convent offers itself; if he can only get them in there, they are provided for for life. There is an end of them. Thus reasons parental love, tinctured with prudence and embittered by many cares."

But, as I need not remind you, neither of these two resources is open to us. Our American women, thank God, have never recruited the ranks of that dismal colony on the borders of Salt Lake, which though American in name is really foreign in the emigration that has peopled it, and as little are American girls prepared to immure themselves within the walls of a convent. What they ask is rather that we shall so widen the sphere of woman that whatever work she can do modestly and well she shall be permitted and encouraged to attempt.

Observe I say not merely well, but modestly. There are some callings from which, as it seems to me, women must forever remain shut out. Any calling which requires conspicuous publicity, masculine activities, and out-door leadership, is not, I venture to submit, for a woman. For one I should not care to see her hanging from a yard-arm, driving a steam-engine, digging in a coal mine, or vociferating in congress. But when we have eliminated from the question those occupations from which healthy self-respect would restrain any really womanly woman, there remain a vast range of employments on which women have not yet entered, but for which, nevertheless, they have singular and supreme qualifications. Already women have acquired the science of telegraphy and they are of course more expert in it than men can possibly be. For what does expertness require in such a calling but a quick ear, and a sensitive touch, and the art of rapid and exact manipulation? And what woman is there who is not superior in all these things to almost any man? And if it be objected that a telegraphic operator has a position of responsibility, and must be a person who can keep secrets, as a woman can not, I answer that experience has demonstrated that the charge is unjust. I remember, when writing a telegraphic message at the window of a New England railway station, that my eye caught that of the young lady operator just as her face broke into a smile. "May I ask at what you are smiling?" I said, with as much dignity as I could command. "O nothing," she replied; "only something that was going over the wires." "But what was it that was going over the wires?" I persisted in demanding—a persistence which was quite in vain. I got nothing in response but a grave shake of the head coupled with an expression as inscrutable as that of the sphynx. In other words, so soon as the sense of responsibility was appealed to, every womanly propensity to tell a secret (if to tell a secret be exclusively a womanly propensity, which I am by no means prepared to admit), retreated into resolute subordination.

But telegraphy is only one of many employments

which may wisely be opened to women. Women are already training themselves to be phonographic reporters. And here again their peculiar aptitudes are a pre-eminent qualification. Why should they not oftener provide for them an honorable maintenance? It was Mr. Peter Cooper, I believe, who, in connection with the recent annual exhibitions of the women's classes of the Cooper Union, mentioned the case of a former student of short-hand reporting in the Institute who, after completing her course, married and removed to the far West. She became the mother of two children, and was living in a happy home, when suddenly all was ended by the death of her husband. She returned to the East penniless and friendless. What was she to do? She bethought herself of her forgotten acquirement—went to work to recall it, and is now earning fourteen hundred dollars a year with her nimble fingers. Why should not those same nimble fingers, coupled with a woman's nice taste and instinctive grace and fluency of execution open to her a score of honorable employments which are now untried? It is a curious and scarcely known fact that in the Middle Ages, the daughters as well as the sons in a family often inherited and carried on the family art or handicraft. When one goes to Nuremberg, or Prague, or Heidelberg, he will find bits of wood carving, artistic work in metal or stone which no modern hand can pretend to rival. How are we to explain this earlier perfection? Simply on this wise: the calling of the father was the calling of the children. Exquisite workmanship was a hereditary trait. "Among goldsmiths the daughters executed chasing, among furniture-makers carving, among stone-masons sculpture, among engravers drawing and graving." Could there be more pleasing or wholesome employment of one's best aptitudes? Contrast the life of a young girl whose days are passed in studying the outlines and reproducing the tracery of some exquisite work of Benvenuti Cellini, with some other whose days, and nights too, are spent in destroying her eyesight and breaking her spirit with the stitch—stitch—stitch of her never resting needle. Why should we deny any modest calling or handicraft, whether behind the counter or in the work-shop, to those whose maintenance and happiness would both alike be found in its pursuit? To this question there is really no answer. Unless we claim that men are a superior caste whose vocations must not be profaned by the entrance upon them of women, there is really no option for us but to proclaim the freedom of labor, and to contend for that freedom until it shall become complete and universal.

And this brings me to the message which I would fain speak to-night to those of you who are so soon to go forth to wider duties and responsibilities of a

life beyond these walls. I might have occupied these
few moments in dwelling upon those fundamental
principles of Christian truth on which that life must
found itself. I might have spoken of the course of
studies which you have pursued here, and the abundant motives and opportunities for continuing such
studies hereafter. I might have spoken of your duties in the home, in the family, in the Church of God.
But there is a much neglected calling outside of these
which yet appeals to you almost more urgently than
any other. It is that calling which I best define by
calling it the duty of woman to women. It is time that
every woman among us, and especially every young
girl with culture and influence and social power, should
awaken to the needs of her own sex. What Deborah
was under the palm-tree at Mount Ephraim every
brave and true-hearted woman is called to be in the
service of as holy a cause and as precious interests.
We call Deborah a prophetess, and so she was. We
regard her as somehow separated by her rare natural
endowments and her exceptionl inspiration, from the
other women of her time, and so she was. But in a
very real and a very living and lofty sense every woman is a prophetess, with a prophet's gifts and a
prophet's calling. For what are prophets' gifts but
that divine insight, that swift and heaven-born intuition which is your rarest gift, your loftiest endowment? It is our province who are men to reach a

consciousness of wrongs to be righted and evils to be remedied by the slower process of reasoning. It is yours to see those wrongs with the more penetrating vision of an often unerring insight, and, not unfrequently, long before men have been awakened to them to burn with a sense of their oppression and their injustice. Shall I be opening an old wound if I say that it was a woman's voice and pen that, more than any other, roused this land to the evils and the cruelties of slavery? and as truly I believe they must be women's voices that must waken us men to the cruelties of that other servitude in which too often and too widely the weak of your sex are to-day oppressed. Do not, then, be afraid to lift your voice in any good cause that aims to elevate women to equal chance and equal respect and equal emolument with men in the great struggle of life. You will be called, many of you, I trust (each one in a separate sphere of domestic happiness and responsibility) to be the "angel in the house." But remember! woman, to be truly the "angel in the house," most resolutely keep and ofttimes use, the wings that raise her above the house and all things in it. You are to do your duty faithfully and lovingly, first of all to those who are nearest to you, but then remember that the woman who in a home thinks only of her own, and lives only for them, will inevitably become a drudge, an idler, or a toy. "No woman can thoroughly order her house, make the wheels of daily life turn without creaking and groaning, adorn her rooms, nay, even design her table, without being a great deal beside a housekeeper, a housemaid, and a cook. It is not by rolling three or a dozen servants into a mistress that a 'lady of the house' can be manufactured. The habits of reason, the habits of mental order, the chastened and refined love of beauty, above all, that dignified kind of loving care which is never intrusive, never fussy, but yet ever present, calm, bright, and sweet, all this does not come without a culture which mere domesticity can never attain."* The woman who is to illustrate these must have learned them by that larger vision which sees beyond her own parlor windows, and which makes her hands and her heart to follow where her eyes have shown her the way.

It is only by widening the range of our vision and by coming in contact with sorrows and wants and perplexities other than our own that we can win the right spirit in which to discharge the duties that lie nearest to us. I turn to that Master whose footsteps, whatever human allegiance may come to be ours, we are supremely called to follow, and nothing is more profoundly characteristic of Him than the breadth of His sympathies for all, and their especial courageous-

* "The Final Cause of Woman," p. 12, 13.

ness and explicitness in the interests of woman. He emancipates her, in one instance, from legal thraldom, in another from hereditary disabilities, in another from social exile, in another from masculine contempt. His words to one who came to Him merely for the healing of the body, "Woman, thou art loosed," are the key to every one of His acts and utterances toward the whole sex. Those acts and utterances are best described by the one word "liberation," and freedom,—freedom from the servitude of a despised inferiority, and the degrading relation of a chattel or a toy is the whole spirit of His Gospel. May God give you grace, my dear young friends, as you go out from the gracious influences of these happy surroundings, to illustrate that spirit in your lives and work. If you see that there are wrongs, injustices, social tyrannies,—and if you will only open your eyes you can not help seeing them,—in the punishments that are meted out to womanly, as distinguished from manly, errors, in the meagre opportunities that are afforded for a woman's virtuous and self-respecting independence, in the indifference that will not bestir itself to cheer and brighten and encourage a working woman's weakness, despondency, and loneliness—then resolve, I beseech you, that it shall be your high privilege to speak for these and to rouse others to speak and strive for them as well. Be, each one of you, a Deborah to cry to some slumberous and sluggish Barak, "Up and do the Master's work, in the spirit of the Master's example!" You remember that legend of Elizabeth the Queen of Hungary, which represents her as having found by the road-side a leprous child whom, dying as it was, she took up in her arms and bore straightway to the ministries of her own chamber and her own couch. And you remember, too, how her sovereign and husband the king hearing of her foolish and maudlin philanthropy, as he accounts it, bursts into the royal bed-chamber to rebuke her for a folly and a temerity which had thus profaned the spot where he himself was wont to repose. As now I recall the story, it tells us that, as the king turned in his anger to fling one glance at the loathsome object, suddenly to his astonished eyes the leper vanished, and in his place there was the form of the divine Christ. It needed not the words which a voice breathed in his ear, "Inasmuch as ye have done it unto one of the least of these, my brethren, ye have done it unto me," to make him read the lesson of the whole aright.

Now, does it need any human words to make us understand the lesson of such an incident to us, who are here to-night? We must remember our brethren, our sisters. You must remember, my dear young friends, the duty of woman to women. May God give you grace and courage both to own and to do it!

You go from these tasks to other and various employments. How long, as you look forward to it, seems the way that stretches before you! And yet how soon and how swiftly it will be ended if your work be done! God bring you to that end with sheaves gathered for His eternal harvest, and when before His throne, you meet the blood-washed throng of ransomed ones, may you hear at least one voice from out that throng say to you, "Not unto thee, O sister, be the glory of the grace that sought and saved me, but unto Him whose love it was that quickened thee and me; but thy hand it was that in my loneliness reached out and clasped fast hold of mine; thy voice it was that cheered and helped and led me; thy pitying, patient, pleading soul of tenderness it was that went out to me, watching and weeping and waiting for me till at last it won me!"

SERMON X.

INSTITUTIONALISM: ITS DANGERS AND FAILURES.

PSALM LXVIII. 6.

"God setteth the solitary in families." *

THE last fifty years have witnessed a remarkable growth of institutional charity, by which is meant, charitable relief administered through the organized and incorporated machinery of institutions. Much of this charitable activity has resulted in very noble and helpful consequences to the poor, the sick, and the degraded. Indeed one can not read such a book as De Liefde's "Romance of Charity," without being tempted to believe that in institutional charity we have found the solution of the whole problem of charitable administration.

If, however, there is much to be urged in favor of such a view, it is questionable whether there is not still more to be urged against it. It will be the object of this sermon, then, to attempt to answer the question how far our institutional charities with their

---

* New York, Feb. 14, 1875.

complex machinery, their rigid organization, and their costly agencies are accomplishing the desired result?

Leaving out the irremediable evils which afflict human society, and which produce those poor which were described when the Master said, "the poor ye have always with you"—how far is modern charity reaching and curing the ills with which it grapples? Among those ills I think we are right in reckoning, with Mr. Greg, in his recent admirable paper on "Realizable Ideals," all the ill health and a large part of the vice and crime which are the direct result of over-crowding, poor food, defective training as to the simplest rules of hygiene, and the absence of every thing that appeals to the higher range of aspiration, or touches and moves the sympathies. We shall always have among us those who have been born blind or crippled or idiotic, though it would be monstrous to pretend that the proportion of these could not be diminished if the general standard of physical vigor and culture could be considerably elevated; we shall always have among us also those whose helplessness is the result of accident, or of epidemic pestilence, or of an orphaned, and abandoned condition—and those too whose miseries and misfortunes are more or less the result of the sins and follies of others. But it will hardly be maintained that a great deal of the sickness, the poverty, the homelessness which daily cry aloud to us for relief, and never more piteously than in times like these, are not remediable, nay, preventable miseries,—miseries which in a different but perfectly attainable state of society need not be. Nor will it be generally denied that a great deal of our present charitable and philanthropic expenditure is innocently, but none the less effectually, operating, to increase and perpetuate the very evils which it undertakes to remedy. The facts are before us, and we can not mistake their import. Side by side with the growth of institutions of charity—hospitals, refuges, asylums, orphanages and the like—rises the growth of a pauperism which is at once the perplexity of the philanthropist and the dismay of the tax-payer. Multiply folds and shelters as fast as we will, the children multiply still faster who are to fill them. Nay, our hospitals, when they are not hedged about by restrictions which make access to them a favor not easily obtained or else only to be expensively purchased, are thronged by ranks of applicants who so press upon each other that the new-comers crowd out the old, ere yet they have attained their convalescence. And other charities, retreats for the aged and the helpless, who that has befriended them does not know that their gravest perplexity is the perplexity how to decide between rival applicants for their scanty benefactions?

Where, now, shall we find the clew to this condition of things? Is it not largely to be found in our forgetfulness of the simple and scriptural principle that "God setteth the solitary in families"? These words affirm, if they affirm any thing at all, that the family is a divine institution, and as such a most sacred, potential, nay, indispensable factor in the upbuilding of society and the welfare of the race. Can any body for one instant doubt it? What is there that has such long centuries to hallow it as the institution of the family? What is it which, long before a Church of God existed, gathered men in that first and simplest worship around the family altar? What is it that no changes of time have been able to eradicate or changes of dispensation improve upon? Nations totter and crumble to their fall. Races are driven hither and thither by the march of conquest and the movements of commerce, but wherever they go, whether it be the English emigrant in the wilds of New Zealand, or the Chinese laborer digging in the gulches of the California coast, straightway out of the confused mass of disorganized and isolated individuals which is flung upon some foreign shore,—straightway the separate atoms begin to crystallize into an inevitable and invariable form, and that form is the human family.

Nor is it surprising that it is so. We may dismiss from our minds any graceful idea of an imaginary home, with only love as its law, and only unselfish and untiring service as its daily rule; we may take the homes which we know as they actually are, with all their frictions, their dissensions, their often forgetfulness of the law of willing self-sacrifice, and as they may be pinched by narrow means, and clouded by sickness, and darkened often by the shadow of a great grief, is there any other spot so sacred, so helpful, so full of repose and courage and sunshine in all God's world? Go ask the people, who, eager for freedom from care, and longing only for indolent self-indulgence, have tried the experiment of living without a home—in hotels, as travellers, as lodgers, as any thing else than parents or children, as heads or subordinates in a household of their own, and if they are candid they will tell you not only how much worry and care they have spared themselves, but also, how, in the process of that economy, the best instincts, the tenderest feelings, the truest joys of human life had somehow been quenched in their breasts or vanished out of their horizon. "God setteth the solitary in families," and it is at his own bitterest cost that any soul among us undertakes to go above His way or to evade or despise His divine order.

The impulse is quite natural which at this point will say that all this is the merest truism, and that it in nowise touches the matter of our charities. But let us look a little closer. Our charities aim to reach and relieve two classes; first, those who are already in homes, and second, those who are without them,—orphans, waifs, the aged and the like. Let us take them separately for a moment.

I. There is a large class of persons who habitually live in homes, and who ordinarily make little or no demand upon our charities. But when sickness comes, or when accident befalls the head of the household, then the daily wage is stopped and the pinch begins. Add to this that some half-dozen people are crowded into a meagre tenement consisting of only two or three rooms—that the sick person can have little privacy and only the most ignorant nursing, and straightway there arises the necessity for a hospital. We must have institutions whither we can carry our accident-cases, and others whither may be sent the unfortunate victims of contagious diseases. In any home, and especially in a poor man's home, it is simply impossible promptly to command perfect quiet, skilful medical attendance, needed apparatus and intelligent nursing, and so the necessity of the hospital seems obvious and imperious enough.

Within certain very definite limits we may unhesitatingly grant it. We shall in all probability, always need institutions to which some mangled laborer, some fever-stricken or infected sufferer may be borne; but what shall we say of the ordinary maladies of human life,—the diseases that are not contagious, the mishaps that are not immediately critical? The first answer of most persons would probably be that the best thing even in such cases, would be to send the patient to a public institution. There is not one of us who can not recall some such institution, where the excellence of its system, the purity of its atmosphere, the skill of its physicians, the orderly stillness of its wards, promise, apparently, far more in the direction of recovery than we should be prone to hope for in the dwellings of the poor. We recall the often fetid air, the confusion, the bungling incompetency even of the most well-meant handling of ignorant relatives or neighbors, and we hail the hospital as an inexpressible boon to the poor.

But just at this point there enters a fact which no one cares much to dilate upon, but which is easily demonstrable from most abundant evidence. It is a fact which so contravenes all our accepted methods of serving the sick poor that it is not surprising that we are unprepared to admit it, and reluctant to talk about it. But it is a fact which it is idle to deny, and almost criminal to ignore. It is this: that a careful comparison of the statistics of great hospitals in great cities in both hemispheres with the statistics of mortality in tenement houses, in those same cities, is not on the whole favorable as arguing increased chances of recovery from hospital treatment. In other words, people do not get well more rapidly, more certainly, or in a larger proportion, whether treated for ailments or for accidents when they are treated in a hospital than they do when they are treated in very inferior homes. We may not, it is true, forget the fact to which attention has lately been called—that this is owing in no inconsiderable measure doubtless, to the imperfect or rather mistaken construction of hospitals, by which their very walls and corridors are made to perpetuate disease, and to pass on a subtle form of hospital poison to those who are so unfortunate as to come within its influence. Nor may we forget, that it is generally believed, if it has not already been demonstrated, that a simpler, less costly and less permanent style of hospital construction will greatly reduce the death-rate whether in fever, surgical, or general hospitals:—so far reduce it, indeed, as to make the chances of recovery decidedly better than those in a tenement. But it is only right to remind those who draw hasty conclusions from this point, that we have no adequate materials for such conclusions until we have found out what will be the result of equally improving the character of our tenement houses. It is one of the most discouraging evidences of a determination, on the part of our great capitalists in this country, to keep the question of their business and their religion quite distinct, that no rich man * has been yet found willing to try the effect of putting within the reach of our poorer classes, decently constructed and adequately lighted, drained, and ventilated homes. As a consequence of this, our tenement houses are often a disgrace to our modern civilization, and the consequences of their ill-construction are dreary enough; *e. g.*, twenty per cent, it is said, of the children born in the basements of such houses are born deformed. Make them fit—simply fit—for the uses to which they are put, erect structures with some slight reference to the fact that they are to be inhabited by human beings and not used to pack men and women like smoked herring, and we need not fear but that the diminished death-rate in our tenements would fall side by side, if it did not fall far more rapidly, in comparison with the death-rate of the most novel and perfect hospital.

And this for a reason which is not far to seek and which lies imbedded in the constitution, and is inherent in the ongoing of the family. The most potent medicine in any human ailment is human sympathy; and that medicine is not for sale by apothecaries. Explain it how we will, there is some-

---

* To this remark the noble and eminently successful work of Mr. Alfred T. White, of Brooklyn, N. Y., forms a signal and honorable exception.

thing in the most bungling ministries of the meanest home, which, in struggling with disease or facing suffering, is calculated to give a sick man heart. He is in an atmosphere in which he is not a mere patient with only a number to distinguish him and a ticket to describe him. His home does not sacrifice hi. personality, and the physician who comes to him is some one who, more probably than otherwise, is at once intimate in his dwelling and confided in by his household. He has not come, primarily, to study him as a scientific illustration, incidentally, to prescribe for his disease. Those about him are not hired nurses, but his own flesh and blood. They may be a very "poor lot" as a tramp once described his wretched wife and wolf-like children, but, in his expressive phrase, they are "kith and kin." If any body on earth has an interest in his recovery they have. And therein lies a more potent spell to heal disease than any medicine that science can devise or utmost skill administer. In the vast majority of instances, the great thing with one who is ill is to put not merely strength into the wasted frame, but courage into the despondent heart. Is it necessary to say that no machinery can do that—nothing save the mighty ministry of love, however ignoble its signs or lowly its instruments?

And therefore, if we would heal the sick we must do it not by multiplying institutions, but by multiplying and ennobling homes. Of course it is a more difficult and a larger task, and this will naturally operate to hinder its being attempted. When we find a miserable home, it is easier to take the sufferer who may be in it, and remove him from his surroundings. This is at once the quickest, the cheapest (or apparently the cheapest), and least painful process. But it is not the surest and the most helpful one. For not only is it questionable how much is gained by the sick person who is removed, it is still more questionable whether we have not inflicted a deeper injury upon those who remain. The increasing facility with which those who would otherwise take care of their own sick and helpless ones roll off such burdens upon societies and institutions is one of the most melancholy features of our modern society. It is an easy education in the worst and most heartless form of selfishness, and the nation which encourages it may retain the name of Christian, but will erelong cease to deserve it.

But what then, it may be asked, is to be done, when sickness and poverty go hand in hand? Are we to leave men to die in their garrets and cellars, because we may do somebody else harm by lifting them out of them? God forbid! We are to go to them in their garrets, and brighten them by our presence, and better them with our money and time and knowledge, all used to lift them up right where

they are. We are to ennoble the home, not to
ignore it; we are to conserve the family, not to dis-
band it; we are to recognize, in one word, that the
household is God's own order, and that it is at its
peril that society tampers with its constitution or
disesteems its enduring sanctity.

II. Very well, it may be said at this point, admitting all this for the moment, you have not touched
a vast range of charities which have grown up among
us, and which have at once a more helpless *clientelle*
and a higher aim. Such institutions are the orphan
asylums, the refuges, the reformatories, which exist,
connected sometimes with our poor-houses and pauper systems and sometimes apart from them. It
may be wise to preserve and elevate the family, and
to strive to make home the most blessed, as it is
certainly the most sacred ministry to the sick, the
destitute, and the infirm; but there still remain those
who have no homes, who have been bereaved of
parents, or, worse still, abandoned by them,—those
from whom by some mysterious providence every
domestic association seems somehow to have fallen
away and left them afloat and alone. In a word
there are the children who are to-day sheltered by
our orphan asylums and gathered in those kindred
institutions whose Christ-like motive has so warmly
enlisted the sympathies of Christian people. Will

any one pretend, it may be asked, that these institutions are a mistake or their work a superfluity?

The question suggests a distinction which it is timely to insist upon. By the sea-side in England the traveller will often find the simple structures which have been reared by the forethought of the Humane Society. They are provided with every apparatus for the rescue of drowning persons and with every means for their restoration. Nobody would dream of dispensing with them, and as little, it is to be presumed, would any body dream of living in them. In other words, they are meant to meet a merely temporary necessity, and as soon as their purpose is accomplished their transient inmate is helped and hastened to his home. Even so of those most timely agencies which, ranging themselves along the brink of the swift-rushing current of our modern life, reach down so often, and snatch some young waif just as it is sinking, it may be for the last time, in the waves. God bless those, anywhere and under whatsoever name, who are doing so noble and so much needed a work as this! But I believe that they who administer such institutions would themselves be the first to admit that they ought to be regarded not as an end, but as a means to an end, and that that end should forever be the restoration of the child to some Christian and well-ordered home. Happily for New York, such a scheme can no longer be regarded as an alluring but utterly impracticable dream, for already there has been at work in that city an association which for twenty-five years has been devoting itself with signal wisdom and with extraordinary success to this very work. It has gathered the drift-wood of the young life of a great metropolis year after year into its schools and lodging houses, not to keep them there, but to pass them on to rural homes, scattered all over the land, in which they have grown up to be virtuous and self-respecting members of society, an element of strength and usefulness in the communities in which they live. It is not possible to turn aside in this discussion to eulogize any particular society, but if one would know how some of the most helpless and hopeless elements of a great community may be most successfully dealt with, let him study the history of the New York Children's Aid Society—a society which has found homes for tens of thousands of children, and which is annually enlarging and increasing its blessed work.

Is it asked now, how is it possible by any such means to grapple with or in any measure supersede the work which is at present being done in our own midst for the neglected and homeless through other agencies? The answer to this question is not far to seek. There are to-day in the public institutions of the state of New York fifteen thousand six hundred and sixty-eight children. Suppose now that instead of maintaining these children, as at present, at a large expense and with at the best but very doubtful results as to their moral well-being, it were resolved to place them in families, there would be just one child for every fifty families in the state. Is it unreasonable to suppose that in every fifty families in this commonwealth there is at least one where, with a little effort, a home could be found for one child,—a home which, however inferior relatively it might be, would be positively superior in its training and influence to the training of any institution ?

For just here, unfortunately, we are not speaking at random. Within the past year or two a gifted Englishwoman, having been invited to address herself to the examination of institutions for the shelter and training of children in connection with the English system for the relief of the poor, ndertook the task of tracing out the history of young girls who had grown up in these schools and shelters, and has lately given to the public the results of her inquiries. It would be difficult to exaggerate the painful character of those discoveries, or the shock which they have given to all thoughtful people. The "London Times" and the "Spectator," journals not wont to speak with undue haste, have recognized Mrs. Senior's report as one of the "most valuable contributions ever made to the literature of charitable relief," and as demonstrating the necessity of revolutionizing the present method of dealing with the young. Mrs. Senior's mode of inquiry was, briefly, as follows: she took the names and addresses of six hundred and seventy girls, between the ages of fourteen and sixteen, who had, after having been reared in seventeen schools supported by the public charities of the city of London, been sent out to service. She traced these girls from place to place, the answers to her inquiries becoming more and more disheartening, and so followed them down, down into still lower depths, until many of them disappeared, having fallen lower and lower in a life of sin until at length, in the expressive phrase of police reports, they "dropped out of sight." In detail, the result of her inquiries was, that of six hundred and seventy girls she was able to get what could honestly be called a good report from only seventy-eight, and even then the mistresses of the best girls complained of them as not knowing how to do the work of small families, as being stolid and machine-like and undeveloped as individuals—as being in fact what is known to us as "institutionized" children. Most of the reports ran much as follows: "A. B. In the institution seven years. Untruthful, dishonest, violent, savage; threatened to stab the nurse in the family to which she went. Knew absolutely nothing of house-work. This girl has had five situations since she left this one, and is now in the work-house." "C. D. In the school of an institution over eight years. Dishonest, untruthful, very sullen, very bad as regards house-work, very dirty in all her habits." And thus the dreary catalogue runs on.

We can repeat it if we choose among ourselves. There are young girls in our hospitals by scores, to-day, who have had a similar training and have ended in a similar degradation. When sickness drives them to the shelter of a public institution they come for a little under the hand, it may be, of some sympathizing and pure woman, and the poor battered nature awakens for a moment to a spasm of repentance and upward reaching aspiration. But too often it is too late. The mechanical and soulless nurture of their childhood, spent it may be in some crowded institution thronged with other orphaned and home-less or abandoned waifs like themselves, has failed utterly to awaken in them one tender emotion or one spark of womanly feeling. They could march and counter-march, they could repeat texts of Scripture and prayers and hymns, they knew the ten commandments and it may be the sermon on the mount with parrot-like precision; but no motherly heart had ever made one word of all that they had learned a living and potent reality to them. Let it not be supposed that in stating these facts it is meant to fault the kindness or watchfulness that reigns in any institution of charity among us. Who must not honor the faithful women who, as matrons or teachers, are grappling with these difficult problems in our charitable institutions? But a woman's heart is capable of just so much and no more. God made her to be the mother of half a dozen children, not of half a hundred or half a thousand. And when the sorrows, the childish fears, the inherited tendencies to evil in a score or a hundred children come pressing upon her day after day, what can she do adequately to meet them? Nothing, absolutely nothing. Either she will expend her sympathies upon a favored one or two, or (what is more apt to be the case), finding herself emotionally unequal to so terrible a strain, she will simply eliminate the sympathetic element altogether from her service and perform her routine with machine-like precision and machine-like soullessness.

And what are the results? What inevitably but mechanical obedience and nothing more in the children so trained—the gradual extinction of all that is human and elevating, so that when the institutional pressure is lifted off there is nothing to restrain the girl or boy from going, as speedily as circumstances shall provide the way, "to the bad." Says the report to which I have referred, "The most violent and ungoverned young persons proved often to be those of whose conduct while in institutions the chaplains had unanimously spoken in the highest terms." It is hard to conceive of a statement which could be a more crushing condemnation of the whole system.

Is such a system worth perpetuating and enlarging among ourselves? Doubtless, the time will probably never come when we shall not need orphan asylums and refuges and shelters for children. And there will always be some children so exceptionally depraved that the safety of the community will demand their more or less protracted detention in houses of correction. But as a rule, it is safe to maintain that the law of all right nurture for childhood is the nurture of the home, and that the first question which ought to engage our attention after getting children into some temporary place of refuge, is the question, "How quickly may we get them out again?" God is wiser than we are, and our poor schemes, that seem so clever and comprehensive, are after all, oftener than otherwise, only clumsy blundering in the face of His eternal laws. "What these children really need," says Mrs. Senior in the report to which I have referred, alluding to the children in English institutions of charity, "what these children really need is a little mothering," and elsewhere I find this inexpressibly suggestive and pathetic statement, "There was one child who did not know how to kiss." She doubtless knew how to say the multiplication table and march in step, but no single sign of tenderness or caressing regard had probably been vouchsafed to her in all her conscious experience. When Pharaoh's daughter found the infant Moses, she does not seem to have regarded him as a reason for organizing an institution. She turned to a lowly woman and bade her be to the child a mother. That that woman was that child's mother, is simply a prophecy of what multitudes of women would equally become if we were to imitate the Egyptian example.

But enough. Within the limits of a sermon it is possible only to skirt the circumference of vast questions and suggest the difficulties which they involve. But this at least we are bound to recognize— that our modern charitable machinery is very far from being perfect, and that much of our activity and expenditure is based upon theories which at least are of doubtful soundness. Let us be unwilling to perpetuate them unless sure that they are wise. Above all, let us be unwilling to believe that any system of charity or philanthropy can be deserving of our confidence unless it is operating, slowly it may be, but surely, to elevate the level of our common humanity, to conquer and expel the evil that is in the world, and thus fill up the low places and make straight the pathway of the Son of man.

SERMON XI.

RELATED LIFE.

ROMANS XIV. 7.

"For none of us liveth to himself, and no man dieth to himself." *

IF we would understand such words as these, we want, as nearly as we can, to get back into that strange and unprecedented period of transition which originally provoked them. We want, in other words, if we are to grasp St. Paul's principle, to appreciate St. Paul's circumstances. As far as possible we must transpose ourselves.

If you were in a Mohammedan country you would find that a people who care nothing for Sunday, regard Friday with the deepest reverence. You would find that while you drink wine and eat swine's flesh, they regard both alike with equal aversion and horror. You would find that, while, if a woman, you account it no dishonor to walk in the streets with your face uncovered, it would be, to women there, an indelible disgrace. Now they were differences somewhat like

---

* New York, April 25, 1880.

these, which embarrassed the progress of the early Church. There were numberless rites and customs, licenses and indulgences which had no moral quality in themselves,—for there can be no moral issue involved in the question whether a man nourishes himself with beef or bacon, so long as the bacon is honestly paid for,—which, nevertheless, not moral but religious precepts or traditions had made to be right or wrong. And questions like these, some Christian disciples were tempted hastily to decide by treating them as of no consequence. There were, doubtless, Christians in Rome who ate and drank, and would fain compel their fellows to eat and drink, what had been offered to an idol, simply because having bought and paid for their meat and drink, it appeared to them of no consequence what had been its previous history. In fact, it was of no consequence. But when their conduct, or their coercion of another, pained and stumbled others—when the license which they took innocently, provoked another to take a license guiltily, and to do a thing which he thought wrong before an enlightened conscience had taught him that it was not wrong, then they, too, were guilty, not of countenancing idolatry but of misleading a brother. They might instruct that brother, and so emancipate him from his old prejudices, but they could not say, "I do not care what my brother thinks, nor what he is led to do by what I do. My life is my own. I will live it my way, and let others live theirs their way. I will order my habits and customs to meet my own convictions,—to suit myself,—and leave others to do the same. I will make myself, in one word, the centre and circumference of my moral world." They could say this, implies the apostle, but they could not do it. "For no one of us liveth to himself, and no man dieth to himself."

And thus we see, that though the precept of the text is local, the principle which it states is universal. We gather about the grave of one who is dead, and who, while he lived, withdrew himself largely from contact with men, and so of necessity from the activities of his generation; and we say of him, "such an one lived a very isolated life." No one can remember to have been in his confidence. His occupation was largely a mystery. With any thing serviceable to his fellowmen he had no sympathy, and reached out toward it no helpful hand. As the years went on, he seemed to find a peculiar, though undemonstrative, pleasure in foiling the curiosity of his neighbors. He told nobody his plans, and the world learned them only when he had accomplished them. He found a furtive delight in that childish and generally unsuccessful endeavor which men make to conceal their gains and acquisitions. He went about the streets with a face as inscrutable as the sphynx, and died, finally, as he had lived. And when he died, his contemporaries said, "There was a man who lived entirely to himself." No, he did not! No man can live to himself, though he hide himself in a cell and take the voiceless vow of the monks of La Trappe. That furtiveness and reserve, that coldness and isolation, are as definite a power in the world as the marching of a regiment. When, on the sea, the wind suddenly becomes chill and searching and the fog thickens ahead, when the mercury falls in the thermometer and the commander paces the deck with a face never so anxious before, you know that you are in the neighborhood of an iceberg — though the iceberg hasn't cabled you a message announcing its proximity, nor sent an officer on board to report to you that it is lying off your weather bow. And just so with those moral icebergs—cold, rigid, irresponsive,—who drift to and fro in the seas of our social life. Silent, selfish, unapproachable, they pride themselves upon living entirely aloof from their fellows. They go into company, it may be, and are busy with their business like other men, but they are determined to live to themselves. And yet, they do not live to themselves. They are felt and recognized wherever they go. The air grows chillier whenever they approach. The frost of their selfishness nips the kindly buds of other lives and makes them as barren and fruitless as their own. The very eccentricity of their endeavors to isolate themselves from all contact and sympathy with other lives attracts attention to them, and produces imitators, who imagine that there must be some inner charm to such a life, just because, outwardly, it is so utterly dismal and unlovely.

And if this is so of men who make it their aim to live to themselves, how clearly we see the force of the apostle's language when we look at some character of an opposite type. Here is a man with native sympathies and fine endowments whose life seems to be engrossed in his business or his studies. Grave responsibilities have been thrust upon him, and we are all the time wishing, we say, that he had more leisure for those great public enterprises that so sorely need just such men as he. What a figure he would have been, what an influence he could have wielded, we think, if he could have gotten out of that narrow round which holds him, as it seems to us, to such poor and petty cares. But every one of those petty cares touches some other life, and every irksome routine is discharged in the presence of his fellows. How can you measure what any one of high moral tone and manly and generous instincts is accomplishing under such circumstances as these ? Every other personality that he encounters feels the impulse of his enthusiasm, or is comforted and refreshed by his courageous benignity. The clerks in his office, the partners in his business, the children in his home, the work-people in his shop, the servants in his house—all these are conscious that something warmer and ampler than the starved currents of their own being has flowed into their lives and has cheered and quickened them. Insensibly, every man with any element of nobleness in him becomes an ideal to some other younger life, and its fresh enthusiasm springs into kindlier activities because, somehow, it has been touched and stirred from without.

In a word (for this is the larger truth to which the apostle leads us), all life in man is consistent,—the highest form of it with the lowest—the life of the soul with the life of the nerves. Now, when we come to look at the nervous system we find that it is, as some one has felicitously described it, a "railway with a double track."* Those who have studied the matter tell us that "there are two sets of nerves, those of motion and those of sensation, running side by side." If we should see them dissected we would perhaps suppose them to be intimately blended; whereas in fact, they are entirely distinct, both in their origin and their office. One set of nerves or tracks, brings us the incoming trains,—the tidings and influences from without; the other set of nerves or tracks, dispatches the outgoing trains,—the influ-

---

* Hopkins' "Strength and Beauty," p. 35.

ences and activities from within. To have both these sets of nerves, constantly, steadily, and healthfully doing their duty—to have my eye and my ear and the nerves which are connected with them correctly reporting to me the beauty and the melody that are outside of me; and then to have my lips and hands and every other organ of expression actively and accurately and vigorously transmitting to others the thought and purpose that are within me,—this is life.

But suppose that this double process is arrested and ceases. Suppose that while my nervous system is receiving impressions it has become incapable of expression. Suppose that with a constant stream of suggestions poured into the brain and so into the mind from without, there is no counter-current streaming forth to influence the world outside of me. Suppose, in other words, that all that you have of vital power and energy should be shut up within yourself—that your hand and your voice should refuse to do your bidding and become slowly, or suddenly, dumb and motionless. We know what we should call this. It would be paralysis, and paralysis is simply an incipient form of death.

In other words, that which is not death, but life, —nervous life, physical life,—is virtually impossible without expression, and that expression forever betrays the man that is behind it. In this sense there is something very startling in the profound and significant truth of the apostle's words. There are many men and women who are trying to live to themselves in the sense that they are trying to keep the quality and character of their lives a secret. They do not expect to live without outward activities, but they imagine that they can so order the expression of their life that it shall imply one thing, while they themselves are another. If any one within the sound of my voice this morning is attempting such an experiment, let me exhort him to desist from it as an impossible undertaking. You may seem to be walking one way, but the world will be quick to detect if you are looking another. They will soon find out what brings the throb into your pulse, and the light into your eye. They will discriminate between what you are, languidly, and what you crave, intensely. And therefore your life will be at once a worthier and a happier one, if you frankly recognize that it is the law of your being to betray itself, and so resolve to bring your nature under that mightiest spell which will make this ceaseless but unconscious revelation of yourself worthy of your nobler possibilities and your best affections.

II. But again. What is true of living, declares the apostle, is true of dying no less, for "no man dieth to himself." Does St. Paul mean, here, that a man can not die without betraying himself, and that whatever may have been the nature of one's life, when he comes to his death-bed, his end must needs reveal himself, and so strongly influence others? Much has been spoken and written which would seem to give color to such a view, but it is doubtful whether it is true, and still more doubtful whether it is the apostle's meaning here.

For, after all, the way in which any one of us may end his life, is a very uncertain indication of what that life has been or will be. There is a physical terror of death which a very little experience teaches us is the characteristic of certain timid and sensitive natures, and which, the more devout and blameless the character that is tortured by it, the keener often is its dismay. Again, and on the other hand, there are persons with such force of will, that the acted career which, like a part, they have been playing all along, they play with equal and wonderful composure to the very end. Indeed those whose observation has been the widest and the closest, are often constrained to own that the closing scenes of most lives are but slightly indicative either of their quality or their tendency. It is true that, at such moments there are often wrung from the lips expressions for which others have waited in vain until then; but the significance of death is to be found not so much in the rhapsody, or the equanimity with which it is actually encountered, as in the temper and purpose with which it is contemplated and approached. "No man dieth to himself." Do we understand, we who are living, that this process of life is not single but double, and that every step forward is a progress in decay and an experience of death? We no sooner get any physical power in perfection than it passes on to its decline. There is no young life among us hastening to its maturity, in which the flush of youth is not the foreshadowing of decay. The law that ripens wastes as surely as it perfects. Indeed there is no single point at which you can for one instant arrest the current and say, "this is simply life." That which seems life is no less incipient death, and the worn-out weariness of the octogenarian utters itself, incipiently, in the tired slumber of the child.

It is in view of such a fact, that a man's life becomes chiefly significant. He is acting, from the beginning, with a certainty in view. And, how is he acting? Knowing that he will die, is he using his life as if it were a vestibule or as if it were a terminus? Knowing that he can carry nothing away with him but his character, is he striving for the development of his character, or for the enlargement of his bank account? Conscious that a part of himself will drop away into the grave and a part endure beyond it, is he living for what will perish, or rather for what will last? How, in other words, is he acting in view of that inevitable day when the windows shall be darkened and the noise of the grinders shall cease and when the mourners will go about the streets? For what is it that happens then? We have been too busy, too pre-occupied, too much taken up, it may have been, with dazzling or distracting externals to recognize clearly the character and quality of a life that was being lived, it may be, right alongside of us. Our friend or neighbor had some infirmity of temper or manner that somehow concealed him from us, or made us misread and so misjudge him. But suddenly he falls at our side, and then there comes that expressive pause when we recollect ourselves and him—when all the past somehow pieces itself together and becomes an intelligible and significant whole, and when, behind the petty mannerisms, the superficial vanity, the hastiness, the vehemence, whatever it was that sometimes offended or wounded us, we see the shining track of a luminous and noble life, clear of baseness and selfishness, pure from soil and shame,—earnest and generous and helpful, and, brooding over it all, a child's faith and a Christian's steadfast hope. And, looking back over such a pathway, we realize how "no man," any more than he liveth, "dieth to himself,"—we see how death groups together and garners up the whole bent and drift of the man's career, and, standing over his open grave, we thank God for one more good "example of those who having finished their course do now rest from their labors."

Of course, to such a portraiture there must needs be an opposite. Did you ever think to yourself with a shudder that you were glad some one was dead? Here is a life that has touched nothing that it has not debased. It is rotted clear through, and it stains with something of its own infamy every fellowship in which it moves. There are people with so little instinct of nobleness or goodness—so hard, so grasping, so unscrupulous, that when we hear that they are dead we heave a sigh of relief that so much baseness and corruption is soon to be relegated to its congenial decay.

But the misery of the death of a bad man is that it has so enormous a propagating power. Talk of the poisonous influence of a graveyard! There are walking cemeteries of "dead men's bones and all uncleanness" that make life loathsome with the horror of their corruptions. They may seem clean as the Pharisees in their morals, but they are filled with an inner venom and faithlessness that poisons life and debases goodness and makes a mock of the world to come.

And so I say, when they die we are glad of it, even though their burial galvanizes into new life all the memories of their dreary past.

But it is not of such that I would lead you to

think this morning. There are others, who have scarce ever crossed the line of modest privacy,—men and women, who, at lowly posts and in quiet homes, have done their work and borne their burden, and then, in God's own time and way, have been called to pass on and up to their reward. And these, as they have not lived, neither have they died, to themselves. Their deaths have brought home to us—what their own busy lives and ours have too often left us but scanty opportunity to recognize—how pure and Christlike was the spirit that animated them, and how clear and steadfast was the witness of their Christian walk and conversation. They have done nothing startling, nothing eventful, nothing that the world will know; but as they moved on, they have left behind them a perfume which will make duty easier and heaven nearer, and the world sweeter because, for a little while, they were in it.

One such I think of, as some of you must needs do this morning, with a sorrow not easily uttered.* A week ago she met with us here, and mingled her voice in these services, and knelt in this holy house. At this altar, to which with such devout constancy she had been wont to come longer than I, her pastor, have ministered at it, she knelt with earnest devotion. To yonder font the children whom God had

---

* Mrs. W. A. Ogden Hegeman.

given her were borne in her loving arms, to their baptism. In the benevolent activities of this parish, and in services which reached out in their influence to homes in the remotest parts of the land, she had been alike constant, faithful, and unwearied. In the home in which her presence was a benediction and her voice a strain of sweet and gracious melody she was an element of sunshine, such as none who knew it can forget. And all this she was, with a womanly reserve and a simple and childlike grace, which charmed alike the most familiar and the most indifferent.

And now that this sweet and engaging life for us is ended, can we say that its influence is ended too? Did the cruel and needless catastrophe that smote that gentle heart into such instantaneous stillness kill the power of that life? Ah no! no! Blessed be God, "no one of us liveth to himself and no one dieth to himself." As they gather about his couch to receive his parting blessing, these are the words with which Israel addresses, and, in them delineates, one of his own children. "Joseph is a fruitful bough . . . . whose branches run over the wall." Even so, there are other lives, men and brethren, whose branches run over the wall,—whose beauty and fruitfulness overflow their own narrow bounds and gladden the world beyond them. Such a life we mourn to-day. Such a life may God make yours and mine!

SERMON XII.

OUR DEBTORS.

ST. MATTHEW XVIII. 28.

*" But the same servant went out, and found one of his fellow-servants, which owed him an hundred pence: and he laid hands on him, and took him by the throat, saying, Pay me that thou owest." * *

OVER against this parable of Christ's, stand in the epistle to the Romans, some brief but pointed words of St. Paul's. They are these: "Render therefore to all their dues: tribute to whom tribute, custom to whom custom. . . . . Owe no man any thing, but to love one another."

Are these two passages contradictory, or irreconcilable? At the first glance they seem so. For at the first glance it is evident that an inspired apostle does not regard debt, whether it be national or individual debt as a national or individual blessing, —differing thus from some moderns who are quite clear as to the blessing of both. On the contrary, he forbids debt in language as authoritative as it is explicit. "Owe no man any thing" is a proposition of the most definite meaning stated in the most transparent language. On the other hand, here is this

---

* New York, November 9, 1873.

parable of Christ's, not so precise, nor so manda-
tory, but equally clear in its drift, and equally posi-
tive in its emphasis. And the parable is substantially
a defence of the debtor—nay, more, an indictment
against the creditor even when the creditor is doing
only that which the law strictly entitles him to do.
For if you will read the old Roman law which obtained among Christ's countrymen when He spoke
this parable, you will see that even that seemingly
excessive and unwarrantable cruelty which is described in the language of the text, was authorized
by the terms of the law itself. Those terms gave
the creditor the right to drag his debtor before the
Roman tribunal by the throat; a custom indeed
which, with all our admiration for Roman law, we
have not ourselves perpetuated, but for which there
is precisely as much warrant as for a great many
other legal maxims which still obtain among us.
Here, however, is one who reprobates the custom,
who impliedly rebukes the law, who enjoins not so
much the payment of debts on the part of the debtor
as the forgiveness of debts by the creditor—who
holds up the persistent and relentless creditor for
our warning and our reprobation, and who, gathering up the whole story into one emphatic precept
at its close, commands us to forgive our debtors,
even as the Supreme Creditor of all of us is daily forgiving our debts to Him.

So stand the utterances of Christ and His apostle
seemingly at issue with each other. And yet it needs
only a little reflection to perceive that common
ground between them on which they are both true.
There is a very simple and primary distinction in
the matter of all human indebtedness, between the
duty of the debtor and the duty of the creditor class,
and it is as plain that Christ is speaking to the latter
class as it is that the apostle is speaking to the
former. Upon these former, implies the apostle, there
rests an obligation which is fundamental to the welfare of society and the ongoing of life. No man may
withhold himself from the discharge of any whatsoever obligation save that obligation (of love) which
it is wholly beyond his power absolutely to discharge. So far as the discharge of any obligation
lies within his power, he is to discharge it, cost what
it may, simply because such fidelity lies at the root
of that golden rule of the Master's, " Whatsoever ye
would that men should do to you, even so," not thirty,
or fifty, or seventy-five per cent as much, but " even
so do ye also to them ! " And right here, if the apostle who wrote those words, " owe no man any thing,"
had lived in our day, he would have paused and
preached a sermon on the intolerable cruelty and injustice of those who make times of financial embar-
rassment an excuse for postponing the discharge of
small obligations—persons who curtail no single lux-

ury, who deny themselves no single indulgence, who are really pinched in no single or appreciable way, but who take advantage of their power of social or moneyed position, or of the fears or the weakness of others to neglect obligations which they alike acknowledge and are able to discharge. To such persons, were he alive, I verily believe, the apostle would give a new and stinging emphasis to that command of his; for such indebtedness is at once a meanness and a cruelty, and wherever it exists,— wherever, in other words, indebtedness is the indebtedness of the strong to the weak, of the clever to the simple, of the rich to the poor,—then one finds himself almost wishing that there were some power which could take the skulking debtor by the throat, and with the strong grasp of righteous authority compel from him the last farthing which may be due to his poorer neighbor.

But, as you have seen in the parable of this morning, the emphasis of what Christ has to say is to be found in its message not to the debtor, but to the creditor. If you are a debtor, it is the emphasis of the New Testament everywhere that you are to pay your debt. "Render unto Cæsar the things that are Cæsar's," is Christ's form of that precept which the apostle utters when he enjoins, "owe no man any thing." Debt is misery, bondage, the loss of independence, and with it, alas! too often the loss of a fine conscience, of manhood, of a lofty sense of equity and rectitude and justice. But there are times when a man is a debtor through no fault of his own; there are times, in a word, when every reasonable expectation is disappointed, and when one finds himself powerless to discharge obligations simply because he finds himself bound up in that great net-work of human obligations which go to make up trade, society, nay, human life, itself, and in which he is an unwilling debtor to another, simply because some others are even more unwilling debtors to him.

I. Now at this point it is that there enters the significance of that parable from which I have taken the text. Amidst the ordinary commerce of life there are constantly arising occasions when other men and women fail in their obligations to us. Somehow or other they are our debtors. They have come under distinct obligations to us, and those obligations, for one and another reason, they fail to pay. How now are we to treat such persons? Two lines of conduct lie open before us which are plainly enough indicated in the language of the parable. One of them is that described in the text. Are you a creditor? Very well, then. Take your debtor by the throat (the law allows you to do so), and crowd him hard up against the statute until you have expressed out of him the last jot and tittle that is due to you. That is one course, and if you follow it, no man can say that you have not acted within the limits of absolute legality. It is not a very elevated or engaging rule of life, but that fact, to many minds, is more than counterbalanced by the consideration that it is the rule of life which governs the vast majority of human beings. In a word, disguise it as we may, the first impulse of humanity is to take its fellowman by the throat crying, "Pay me that thou owest!"

Look at the facts for a moment, and see if this is not the case. Of course I am not affirming it merely of those obligations which in a narrower and conventional sense we commonly call debts. Concerning these, perhaps it is less true, than concerning any other obligations. In all commercial transactions between man and man there is a very definite and practical peril in harsh and oppressive exactions which carries its own remedy with it. Ordinarily the creditor has as little interest in ruining his debtor as the debtor has in being ruined, and ordinarily, therefore, the forbearance of a financial creditor is only another name for an enlightened selfishness. But the largest indebtedness of life is not owed or paid in money. It is that complex obligation of justice, of respect, of truthfulness, of honor, which exists between men and women wherever there are human souls and a human society.

There are some things which are forever due from each one of us to the other, and upon the payment or withholding of which more depends than upon all the bank vaults in Christendom.

Now it is with reference to these things, that there exists that wide-spread impulse of humanity to which I have just referred. There are a great many people in the world whose first and last thought in life is of what is due to them. Do you meet them in the ordinary intercourse of daily life? Nothing is more obvious than that they are on the watch to see that they get their dues. There are men in professional life or in public station (and it is particularly the infirmity of those who, like the clergy, are more or less isolated from frequent and familiar intercourse with other men), who are incessantly on the watch to see that they are approached with sufficient decorum and addressed with a proper respect. There are mothers and fathers in families who are so absorbed in the thought of what is due them from their husbands or wives or children, that life becomes a sharp, acrid, microscopic hunt for slights that were never dreamed of, and for discourtesies which no one intended. And when one gets outside of the home there are men and women whose mission in our social life is to breed dissensions and perpetuate differences and resentments by dwelling upon what is due to themselves or theirs, and what has unjustly been withheld by others. There are great griefs in life which we can accept with meekness, and bend to with absolute submission; but there are little wrongs, minor slights, small neglects and injustices behind which often there lingers no deliberate intention nor even any malicious impulse, and these seem to have a power to infuriate us, until, if we do not literally "take" those who have wronged us "by the throat," it is not because we have not a very decided impulse to do so.

And in the indulgence of this aggressive and exacting spirit, there are a great many persons who are quite ready to defend themselves. Such persons are swift to tell you that it is only he who is mindful of his dues, and vigilant as to what others owe to him, who stands any chance in such a world as ours of getting what is simply his right. And these persons are so far borne out in their assertion as this, that as a matter of fact, they ordinarily do get their dues. We all know these relentless creditors of humanity who exact the last farthing, and who never abate an iota of their claims. We have met them in travel, in trade, in the most simple pleasures of life, and in all these relations their intense consciousness of their dues, their persistent assertion of their rights has poisoned the air and embittered the happiness of all around them. Into the most friendly and unreserved intercourse they have dragged a spirit which is perpetually reiterating "Take care! you can not over-reach me. You shall not forget for one single instant what is my due. You shall not cross by a hair's breadth the line of exact and mathematical reciprocity, and if you do, then I am watching to take you by the throat and remind you that not one moment may you forget what you owe to me." And speaking and acting thus, these are they who are more than all others responsible for the strifes and resentments the lingering and long-cherished grudges that deform and disfigure human experience!

But surely, it may be said, there is a time in our dealings with others when we may fully insist upon our dues, and when to forgo such insistence is simply to encourage unscrupulous aggression and dishonesty. Surely, there are some insolent offenders against one's rights whose offences are so rank and grave that simple justice to others, if not to one's self, demands their rebuke. Undoubtedly, and it is the glory of human society, that society itself sooner or later lays its hand upon such offenders and deals with them more justly and summarily than any one individual can possibly do. There comes a time when Shylock's cruel exaction against Antonio becomes the quarrel of all Venice, and when all classes of society and all the powers of the state unite in making the grasping Israelite a warning for all time. But ordinarily the issues that divide us from our fellows are far more trivial than this. When we are most noisily insisting upon our dues, has it ever occurred to us to pause and think how small was the debt which was owing to us? O! could we gather together the claims against our fellow men and women which we have accounted just claims, and concerning which our hearts have burned with resentment and our cheeks flushed with anger—the petty miserable quarrels and heart-burnings about questions of precedence, about some unintentional slight, about the ten thousand ·minor collisions which jar and irk us in life—what a contemptible catalogue it would be! And we who have done so, as often as not profess and call ourselves the disciples of a crucified Christ. Shame on us that we have so poorly learned the lesson of His gospel or the meaning of His cross.

II. For when we come to look at either of these, what is so sublimely significant as the utter absence in them of any clamoring for dues—any insistence on the part of the Saviour of the race of what men owed to Him. It would be worth our while to sit down and read the gospels through, to see if we can find anywhere an instance in which Christ even reminded men of what they owed to Him. There is one indeed, in which at the first glance there seems to be something like the assertion of such a claim, but the moment that we look at it a little closer we see in it only a new and more wonderful illustration of that self-abnegation which is at once the distinction of Christ and the glory of His religion. It is when Simon the Pharisee, having bidden Jesus to his table, is shocked at His familiarity with an erring woman who has literally crawled up to and crouched at His feet and is covering them with her embraces. It is in justification of her that Christ replies to the offended conventionalist, "Thou gavest me no water to wash my feet, but this woman hath washed them with her tears and wiped them with the hairs of her head. Thou gavest me no kiss, but since I came in she hath not ceased to kiss my feet." But we miss the significance of Christ's language here, entirely, if we merely imagine Him to be rebuking Simon's neglect of what was due Him by means of a courteous innuendo. On the contrary, He mentions Himself only to excuse the Magdalene, and it is plain from the beginning to the end of the scene that He is not thinking of what another had owed Him, but rather of what her supreme devotion which so outran all measurement of mere custom or due, had freely given to Himself.

And thus it was throughout His earthly life, with Him to whom the race owes every thing. As He goes to and fro among men, nothing is more characteristic of Christ than His invariable silence concerning what men owed to Him. Even St. Paul sometimes takes his stand upon his rights, and constrains his unwilling enemies to pay to him that respect which was his due as a Roman citizen; but Christ begins and ends His ministry among ungrateful countrymen who from the outset owed Him gratitude, reverence, an eager and whole-hearted welcome; without a murmur of reproach or even a flush of resentment towards those who withheld from Him each and all of these.

And what, now, was the result of it? Was it not that erelong, that wonderful magnanimity, that incomparable forbearance won for Him not the plaudits of a few admirers, but the devotion of a regenerated race? True, men did not take Him and make of Him a King. No august and imperious assertion of His right to rule hewed for Him a way to the throne of Israel, or to the visible sovereignty of His countrymen. But no sooner is He dead, than that power of His life which could not die, erects for Him a throne in the hearts of humanity, and lifts Him to its occupancy forever. That great company of the priests who, so soon after they had crucified Him, became obedient to the faith, what was it that conquered them? Ah! what but that vision of a life which could so absolutely forget itself, its rights, its claims, its dues, in utter and unstinted sacrifice for others!

Believe me, it will always be so. You and I may insist upon our dues, and get them; we may demand our pound of flesh, and no clever quibble of ingenious friendship may be able to prohibit our taking it; we may go through life, and in all its various relations have the comfortable conscious- ness (if it be a comfortable consciousness), that no needy debtor ever escaped out of our clutches, that we were strong enough and tenacious enough to ex- act the last dollar, the last tittle of due custom or honor or respect. And after all, what will it all be worth? Here, over against us is one who has more than once waived his just claims, and forgiven an- other his debt. Aye, here is one,—I thank God in these searching times there are many such,—who has lifted off the hard hand with which he might have crushed his brother man, and has rather borne and been patient with him. Aye! here are men and wo- men the world over who in the home, and the family, in their pleasures as in their duties, amid the thousand strifes and rivalries that enter into life, have not in- sisted upon their dues; but, remembering how One to whom they owe so much, has been most patient and tender with them, have striven to translate that same patience which they have learned of Him into for- giveness and forbearance towards others. They may not get the most money, or the best places, or the most obsequious salutations. But these are the men and women whom humanity will carry on its lips and in its heart. Theirs it will be, and ours too, if ours shall be that spirit of the Master which has inspired them, to discover that the best payment is the heart's gratitude and devotion and love,—that payment which is the best, simply because it can never be exacted, but only freely given.

Shall we not remember this? The time will not be a great while in coming, when these active brains and these busy hands and these resolute wills of ours will lie down in that last struggle which ends in stillness and the grave. And when that moment comes, and the flickering life hovers between two worlds, will it comfort us then, think you, to remember those whom we pressed to the uttermost here, wringing from them our dues with stony indifference to their cries? Nay, rather let me ask you when, in that supreme moment, our last straining gaze searches for the form of One to guide us in the darkness, shall it be ours to hear from lips that once quivered in anguish for our sake, "I forgave thee all that debt . . . couldest thou not have had compassion on thy fellow-servant, even as I had pity on thee?"

SERMON XIII.

"OWE NO MAN ANY THING."

ROMANS XIII. 8.

"Owe no man any thing, but to love one another." *

WE can not return to such a feast as that which
assembles us in this place this morning without
thoughts that revert to its origin, and to the circumstances which gave to it its character. I speak
to those whose lineage traces its way back to various
sources—English, Scotch, Dutch, French and German. But there is no one of us, however remote our
ancestries from one another, who does not feel that we
have nothing more distinctively American than this
day, and that however peculiarly New England like
many of its original characteristics may have been,
i. is the relic of an age and a spirit which belonged
in greater or less degree to all our forefathers alike.

That spirit disclosed itself in certain conspicuous
characteristics which stand out in strong relief. As
we read the history of our ancestors, whether they
were the founders of New England or the founders of

---

* New York, Thanksgiving Day, 1877.

the New Netherlands, we find it distinguished everywhere by energy, probity, frugality and domestic concord. Underneath the charming pictures which Irving has drawn in his "Knickerbockers' History of New York," you may trace the influence of that earlier, simpler age of which he there tells the story. The old burgher and his frau, the primitive and orderly habits of the house and the people, the universal contempt for trickery and equivocation, the sturdy virtue that scorned a dishonest advantage, and hated debt as the worst of slaveries,—the family unity that bound the household, master and servant, husband and wife, parent and child in a common industry, unity, and economy, these are the lineaments of that earlier life which laid the foundations of this New York of ours and opened the avenues of its future prosperity. If we should be bidden, to-day, to keep a thanksgiving now as our fathers kept it then, we should doubtless smile with a fine sense of superiority at the contrast which our own homes and habits would usually present. "The fireplace of patriarchal dimensions," so Irving has sketched the scene, "gave welcome to the whole family, old and young, master and servant, black and white; nay, even the very cat and dog enjoyed a community of privilege and had each a right to a corner." The elders smoked their long pipes and conversed in brief sentences, with long pauses between. The mother spun or knit, and the youngsters gathered in their own corner listening to some chronicler who told the story of still earlier and sterner times. In those homelier days a well-regulated family always rose with the dawn, dined at eleven, and went to bed at sunset. Dinner was a private meal, and the social gatherings began at three in the afternoon and ended before six. The old Dutch china was passed on from generation to generation, and the viands upon the table and the garments upon the persons of the guests gave scant token of elaborate forethought or unusual cost. Imagine, now, if you can, that to some such homely festivity we should be bidden to-day. How mean and even vulgar it would all seem! How tasteless and even wearisome we might easily account it! And yet these things were the expressions of the social and domestic life of a people who lived resolutely within their means, who neither ate nor drank nor wore what they had not paid for, whose life was no miserable struggle to escape from tradesmen and creditors—who were bitten by no tarantula madness to rival the extravagances and imitate the fashions of foreign life, who feared God, and obeyed the law and bred in their children the same virtues.

And as of these, so of those others, our New England ancestry from whom many more among us, here gathered this morning, are doubtless sprung. They lie to-day, sleeping among their own austere northern hills, beneath the shadow of the white clapboard meeting-house, and too often, I fear, we shall look in vain for their successors. Among them were men whom Horace Bushnell aptly calls "the sturdy kings of homespun, who climbed among the hills with their axes to cut away room for their cabins, and for family prayers, and so, for the good future to come. Among them were others who foddered their cattle on the snows and built stone-fence while the corn was sprouting in the hills; getting ready in that way, to send a boy or two to college. Among them, too, were housewives that made coats every year, like Hannah, for their children's bodies, and lined their memories with the Westminster Catechism. Among them were the millers and the coopers, the smiths and the joiners, the district committees and the school-mistresses, the road-masters and the deacons, and withal a great many sensible, wise-headed men, who read a weekly newspaper, loved George Washington and their country, and had never a thought of going to the state legislature. These were the men that made New England," and that have sent forth their descendants throughout the length and breadth of this broad land. How simple, nay, how even severe, as it seems to us, were their modes of thought and habits of life and customs of recreation. There must be some here who have memories of those plain New England homes, and of the men and manners that adorned them. There was simplicity, there was drudgery, if you choose, but there was health and virtue and integrity. "Facing all weather, cold and hot, wet and dry, wrestling with the plough on the stony-sided hills, digging out the stones with hard lifting and persistent prizing, dressing the flax, threshing the rye, dragging home in the deep snow the great wood-pile for the winter's consumption, they knew no tedium and no discontent. And even so the mothers spent their nervous impulse through their muscles, and had so much less need of keeping down the excess or calming the unspent lightning by doses of anodyne. In the play of the spinning-wheel they spun fibre within, and wove daily something strong and wholesome in the pattern of womanly love and service. But, best of all, around all this simpler life there was a closely girded habit of economy. Harnessed all together, into the producing process, young and old, male and female, from the boy that rode the plough-horse, to the grandmother knitting under her spectacles, they had no conception of squandering lightly what they had won so hardly.

And yet, they had their ways and hours of recreation, and, dry and angular as their life now seems to us, brightened it often with mirth and good cheer. Who that has ever seen an old-fashioned New England fireside or heard its story from some one who long ago had a place beside it, will ever forget it ? The home circle, gathered about the huge fireplace, the sleigh load of guests from the neighboring village, the quaint old songs, the chairs set as wedges in some huge periphery of mirth and good feeling, the elders discussing the minister's sermon in one corner, and scenting a heresy with a keenness which had at least the virtue that it cared for the difference between truth and error, the simple fare and simpler furniture, the old Bible brought reverently to be read before the friends withdrew, the hymn sung to Coronation or Duke Street, or old Warwick, the homely prayer, with its unpolished phrase and rugged fervor—it was thus that our fathers, some of them, kept their thanksgiving days and rounded the quiet lives of which those days were so cherished and conspicuous a feature ! Here again, there is a fine field, if we choose to enter it, for our more modern scorn or criticism. How narrow and intolerant, and even full of cant sometimes were those earlier and hardier worthies ! What stern and even cruel ideas they had about God and little children and the unpardonable quality of sin ! Well, there were some sins that they did find it hard to forgive. Sins against home and kindred, sins against common honesty, sins of extravagance and self-indulgence, of ungoverned ambition and personal unfaithfulness—upon these they had certainly but scant and stinted mercy. But they paid their debts and kept their word. They ruled their own houses and had their children in subjection. A household then was a united and homogeneous community, in which the love and trust that reigned within were prophecies of the peace and contentment that were shed abroad. If it was rugged, that elder American life of ours, at least it was on the whole healthy and upright and kindly.

But at any rate, whatever may have been its characteristics, we are far enough away from them now. No nation in the world has ever known, I venture to affirm, so radical a revolution in its social and domestic habits as has this people, in so short a space of time. During the last fifty years the growth of wealth in the United States has undoubtedly been a growth of almost unexampled rapidity and of wide-spread diffusion. The enormous tide of emigration, only of late beginning to be materially checked or retarded, the extraordinary development of mineral and agricultural resources, the discovery of gold in California and of silver in Nevada, the multiplication of our manufactures and the daring and enterprise of our commerce, have, in one way or another, made all the world pay tribute to a nation barely a century old. And, side by side with this increase in wealth and population, in productive energy and in material resources has gone an equally remarkable growth in facilities of intercourse and frequency of communication with the remotest nations and capitals. Under favorable circumstances nine days will put the traveller in London, ten in Paris, twelve in Vienna, and fifteen in Alexandria. But this can not be without a converse facility of which we do not so often think. Less than a fortnight will bring to us the fashions and the follies, the amusements and the extravagances of the most distant capital in Christendom. And in no soil in all the world do those fashions and extravagances take a quicker root or have a more rapid growth than in our own. So that it has come to pass that while our vices and follies, our ostentation and prodigality, if we originate any, are slow to make their way beyond our own borders, the irrational excesses of other peoples too often find among us eager and cordial welcome.

I believe that De Tocqueville has pointed out the explanation of this with equal precision and discrimination. In contrasting a government which includes a hereditary aristocracy with our own, he observes—"Amongst a nation where an aristocracy predominates in society and keeps it stationary, the people in the end get as much accustomed to poverty as the rich to their opulence. The latter bestow no anxiety upon their physical enjoyments for they have become possessed of them without effort, and can lose them without dismay. All the revolutions which have ever shaken or destroyed aristocracies have shown how easily men accustomed to superfluous luxuries can do without the necessaries of life,"—while on the other hand "those who have never tasted such luxuries do not torment themselves with the thought of things that are hopelessly beyond their reach." When, however, the distinctions of ranks are confounded together and class privileges are destroyed, there is kindled in men's hearts a very different sentiment. "Many scanty fortunes spring up; those who possess them have a sufficient share of physical qualifications to conceive a taste for such pleasures, but not enough to gratify that taste. They rarely procure them without exertion; they never indulge in them without apprehension. They are therefore always straining to pursue or to increase gratifications so delightful, so imperfect, so fugitive." *

"If," he adds, "I were to inquire what passion is most natural to men who are stimulated and circumscribed by the obscurity of their birth and the mediocrity of their fortune, I could discover none more peculiarly appropriate to their condition than this love of physical prosperity. The passion for physical comforts is essentially a passion of the middle classes; with those classes it grows and spreads; with them it preponderates. I never met, however, in America with any citizen so poor as not to cast a glance of

---

* "Democracy in America," vol. ii. p. 156.

hope and envy on the enjoyments of the rich, or whose imagination did not possess itself by anticipation of those good things which fate still obstinately withheld from him. . . . . . The love of physical comforts is now become the predominant taste of the nation; the great current of human passions runs in that channel, and sweeps every thing along in its course."

These words were written nearly fifty years ago (1833), and if they were true then, it will hardly be pretended that they are less true now. The love of display, the craving for luxuries, the eagerness to have and wear and eat and drink what one's neighbors have and wear and eat and drink, the wide-spread disposition to make life more ornate and less rugged, more smooth and less self-denying; these are tendencies and desires concerning which there can be no dispute nor any serious question. Explain it as you choose; say that the austereness of the fathers has provoked the luxury of the children; appeal to the age as placing greater luxury within easy range of a greater number,—the fact remains that, on the whole, our habits are not simple, our training is not frugal, our social customs are not plain nor inexpensive.

Such a fact might surely be regarded with something of solicitude if it indicated no more than the advent of an age of self-indulgence. For, whatever may be said in favor of profuseness and luxury, it will not be denied that luxury is enervating. We do not need to go back to Rome to see that national luxury paved the way for national dishonor. France discovered it in the reigns of the Louises. England experienced it in the time of Charles. Costliness of living and unlimited personal indulgence mean enfeebled manhood and decaying intelligence.

But, in our case it means something more and worse. It means the growth of a relaxed sense of individual honor and of common honesty. It means a disposition that will have luxuries by paying for them if it can, but which will have them anyhow. And so with us, such an age has come to mean an age in which the mere externals of living have become so precious to some persons that, rather than forfeit or forego them they will betray a trust and defraud a creditor. To think lightly of debt, and the personal and business discredit which comes or ought to come with it, to be loose in matters of trust, and reckless or unscrupulous in dealing with the interests of others, to maintain a scale of living which is consciously beyond one's means, and yet to go any lengths and run any risks rather than abridge or relinquish it, these things are so frequent, if not so familiar, as almost to have lost the power to shock us.

And yet is there any degradation more abject, any slavery more absolute than they are sure inevitably to involve? Every now and then the community stands aghast at some tragedy of horror in which a poor wretch, daring rather to face his Maker than his creditors, jumps off the dock or blows his brains out. A dozen of his fellows, hastily gathered and as hastily dismissed, register their verdict of "suicide occasioned by financial difficulties" and the great wave of human life rolls on and over, and the story is soon forgotten. Whereas, if we fairly realized what such things meant, we would empanel as the jury, every youth who is just setting out in life, every husband who has just led home a young wife, every woman who is a mother or a daughter in so many thoughtless households, and cry to them "See! Here is the fruit of extravagant living, and chronic debt. Here is the outcome of craving for what you can not pay for, and of spending what you have not earned. Would you be free and self-respecting and undismayed, no matter how scanty your raiment or bare your larder? Hear the apostle's words to that Rome that had such dire need to heed them, 'Owe no man any thing, but to love one another.'"

Yes, honest dealing and mutual love. Believe me, the two things are closer together than we are wont to imagine. Said a foremost physician in one of our foremost cities not long ago, when asked how far the facility with which American constitutions break down, was occasioned by overwork, "It is not overwork that is killing the American people: neither the people who work with their brains nor those who work with their hands. I see a great many broken-down men and broken-down women. I am called to treat scores of people with shattered brains and shattered nerves, but they are not the fruits of overwork. The most fruitful sources of physical derangement and mental and nervous disorders in America, are pecuniary embarrassments and family dissensions."

For, as I have just intimated, far oftener than we imagine, the two things lie close together. The father, crowded beyond endurance by the strain to maintain a scale of living long ago pitched too high, the mother consciously degraded by the petty evasions and domestic dishonesty that draws money for wages or marketing and spends it for dress; the sons and daughters taught prodigality by example, and upbraided for it in speech,—what can come to such a home or family circle but mutual recrimination and personal alienation and chilled and embittered feeling? How can love reign in a household where mutual confidence and mutual sacrifices, where the traits that inspire respect and kindle affection are equally and utterly wanting? It seems as if it were a matter extremely remote from any domestic or social interchange of the affections whether two people or indeed a whole community made it a rule to pay their debts; but in fact, not to pay one's debts is as sure and as short a road as can be found to the extinction of confidence, the destruction of respect, and the death of love.

Where now shall we look for a corrective? I answer, in a higher ideal of the true wealth and welfare of the nation, and so of the individuals who severally compose it. It was Epictetus who said, long ago, "You will confer the greatest benefit upon your city not by raising the roofs, but by exalting the souls of your fellow-citizens, for it is better that great souls should live in small habitations than that abject slaves should burrow in great houses."* The words send our thoughts back again to those memories of our forefathers with which I began this discourse. Recall for a moment their simple beginnings. "They brought hither in their little ships," as some one has described them,† "not money nor merchandize, nor array of armed force, but they came freighted with religion, learning, law, and the spirit of men. They stepped forth upon the shore, and a wide and frowning wilderness received them. Strong in God and in their own heroic patience they began their combat with danger and hardship. Disease smote them, but they fainted not; famine stalked among them, but they feasted on roots with a patient spirit. They built a house for God, and then their homes for themselves. They established education and the ob-

---

* "Fragments," lxxvi. † H. Bushnell.

servance of a stern but august morality, and then
legislated for the smaller purposes of wealth and
convenience. They gave their sons to God; through
Him to virtue; and through virtue to the state. So
they laid the foundations. . . . What addition,
we are now tempted to ask, could any amount of
wealth or luxury have made to the real force of these
beginnings? Having a treasure in her sons, what is
there besides, whether strength, growth, riches, or
any thing desirable, which a state can possibly fail
of? Wealth is but the shadow of men; and lordship
and victory, it has been nobly said, are but the pages
of justice and virtue."

> "What are numbers knit
> By force or custom? Man who man would be,
> Must rule the empire of himself; in it
> Must be supreme, establishing his throne
> Of vanquished will, quelling the anarchy
> Of hopes and fears, being himself alone!"

And this is what, in their frugal lives, their sturdy
implicity, their honest dealings, our fathers taught
us. As we remember, on such a day as this, how
much we have to thank them for, as well as to
thank God for, let us resolve that we will not be
unworthy of a lineage so noble, a race so true. In
those questions of the hour which are so much the
echo of the questions of our personal conscience, let
us lift up our voices for the payment of every honest

debt in honest coin. Let us resolve that, so far as in us lies, the nation shall have a clean and righteous record in its dealings with those who, whether here or there, are its creditors; and, that this may come to pass, let us begin by dealing justly with those creditors who are ours. Let us pay every debt but the debt which we can never wholly pay, whether to God or our neighbor,—which is the debt of love. But let us gladly own that debt, and be busy, every day of our lives in making at least some small payment on account. As we gather about the family-board to-day, let us remember the houseless and homeless and unbefriended, and be sure that we have done something to make sunshine in their hearts, no matter what November gloom may reign without. And as we grasp the hand and look into the eyes of friend and kinsman, be this the greeting that we give, "Brother, whatever else our homes provide, to-day, of plenty and good cheer, 'let us provide things honest in the sight of all men,' and then, in the name of that Master whom we serve and who has loved us with such a great, exceeding love, 'let all bitterness and wrath, and anger, and clamor, and evil speaking be put away from us, with all malice; and let us be kind to one another, tender hearted, forgiving one another,' whatever the old wound that aches and burns to-day, 'even as God for Christ's sake hath forgiven us!'"

SERMON XIV.

FAITH IN GOD AND MAN.

PSALM CXVI. 10.

"I believed and therefore will I speak; but I was sore troubled: I said in my haste, All men are liars." (Prayer Book Version.) *

THERE is something most affecting in the mental struggle which these words reveal to us. If the psalm in which they occur is a fragment of David's personal experience, then they find in that experience the clew to their meaning. Criticism has much disputed concerning them, and with but meagre success; but when we brush away the dusty lore of the schools and feel beneath for the beating, in these words, of a human heart we straightway find it, and come to understand their meaning. The psalm is the cry of a man torn by doubts, but not conquered by them. It is the voice of one who has been down into the deep waters and for a time has lost his footing. "The snares of death compassed me round about, and the pains of hell gat hold upon me. . . . . . . O Lord, I beseech thee deliver my soul! I shall find trouble

---

* New York, Jan. 27, 1878.

and heaviness, but I will call upon the name of the
Lord." And then, as the clouds begin to break, and
the light begins to dawn, "Gracious is the Lord and
righteous: yea, our God is merciful: the Lord pre-
serveth the simple: I was in misery and He helped
me. Turn again then unto thy rest, O my soul!"
Come back, O tempest-tost wanderer, seeking peace
and shivering in the dismal sense of loneliness and
doubt, "turn again unto thy rest, for the Lord hath
rewarded me. And why? Thou hast delivered my
soul from death, mine eyes from tears and my feet
from falling!" And then, as the whole consciousness of the man wakes up out of the hideous dream
of distrust and despair in which he has been walking,
he breaks forth into that sublime assertion of his faith
and trust, "I will walk before the Lord in the land of
the living. I believed and therefore have I spoken;
but I was sore troubled; I said in my haste, All men
are liars!"

Can we not understand it now? Time was when
with this man, David, nothing was true. He had had
in the treachery and enmity of Saul a cruel experience
of human perfidy. The man who owed to him the
safety of his throne had hunted him like a wild-beast
and striven to trap him like a fox. For a time every
one, every thing had seemed to be against him. And
he had believed that things were against him. He
had lost his faith alike in God and in man. There

was no truth, nor goodness, nor justice any more in the world. And in his despair he says so. "All men are liars!" he cries, and when he does so he means to include God and men together. He believes as little in the One as in the others. Every thing is false and hollow and treacherous, and he himself is the sport of a cruel and heartless destiny.

But with calmer moments comes a juster vision. This outlaw remembers more than one time when, black as the outlook seemed before him, there broke upon his eyes a ray of light. He was in misery and help did find him. He was in the snare of death itself, and somehow a hand reached down and disentangled the meshes of the net and set him free. Looking back now, he could recognize that hand. It was God's. And if God was not false, men were not. They were, after all, something like the Being who had made them. Some among them might be treacherous, but it was in his haste that he had said that "all men are liars."

It is of the spirit which betrays itself in such an accusation as that, and of the tendencies which are involved in it, that I propose to speak this morning. It has been left to a pitiful cynicism and to a threadbare wit to remind us, especially of late, that if David had lived in our days the words which he once uttered in haste he might now have spoken with utmost deliberation. Is it true? Is truth an extinct species in the

moral universe ? Is falsehood the invariable characteristic of the dealings and the speech of men ? I will
not trifle with your intelligence by seriously discussing
the question. I will summon to the witness-stand
every perjured man and woman in all the land. I will
rake the kennels and the jails for those who, of whatever rank or class or calling, have been false to their
promises or their oaths. I will recall all the dreary
catalogue of social or domestic or commercial or political falsehood to vows and covenants and plighted
faiths in whatsoever scandal-hunting sheet of whatsoever vilest authorship these crimes may have regis-
tered, and in the face of all of them I will not hesitate
to affirm that on the whole, the standard of truth is
not lower, but higher, and the plighted faith of man
not a less sacred, but a more sacred, thing than ever
before. We seem to forget, when we sit down to form
a judgment of this matter that the record of a city's
or a nation's crimes is not the history of its people.
A man goes to the brink of yonder river and standing
where a sewer discharges its foul and feculent con-
tents into the stream, dips up a bucketful and cries,
"This is a specimen of the waters of the Hudson." Is
it ? All day long and all year round that stately
stream has been gathering the crystal products of a
thousand mountain springs and forest streams and
bearing them in steadfast silvery splendor to the sea.
And those pure and sparkling waters, running in their

broad and ever deepening channel, not some dirty eddy fouled by a city's nameless filth, are the source from which you are to seek a specimen of the waters of the Hudson. Even so of that civilization of which many of us are tempted to think so poorly. We may not blink or belittle the crimes that are done in high places or in low ones—least of all may we deny the essential evils from which those crimes have sprung; but to own the power of evil in the world, to be afraid of it, to hate it, to frown upon its exhibitions when they flower into personal transgression—that is one thing. It is quite another to be precipitated by these things into that blunder of hasty generalization which David no sooner detected in himself than he so simply and manfully disowned and repented of it.

For such a habit of misjudgment is not merely a blunder, it is worse : it is a cruel and often soul-destroying wrong. We are fond, just now, of dwelling upon the evils which result from over-confidence in others, and are wont to speak sternly of the falsehoods which have repaid with wrong and treachery an unsuspecting trust. Undoubtedly there are such instances, but there are many more concerning which no such language is in any wise appropriate. There are a great many instances in which the crimes of others are only a little less chargeable to our carelessness than to their criminality. "Study to be quiet and mind your own business," enjoins the apostle, but

if in our indolence or pre-occupation, we choose to
neglect our own business, we may not refuse to share
the blame with those whose trust was not theirs only,
but ours also. No one of us has a right, by neglect
of his own duty, to thrust upon another an over-
whelming temptation to wrong-doing and then wonder if in some moment of desperate perplexity that
other yields to it. There is a wise and righteous
caution born not of suspicion but of justice and of
love, which is widely different from distrust.

But when this is said, we may not forget that caution and watchfulness in our dealings with our fellowmen are one thing and utter faithlessness in their
truthfulness or integrity quite another. Have we ever
realized that, if we seriously believed as some of us
are willing to affirm, that all men are liars, life would
be simply unendurable? After all, the foundations
of human society are laid in the cement of mutual
trust, not of mutual suspicion. It paralyzes effort,
it deadens aspiration, it destroys hope when we find
that our own confidence in others evokes no answering trust from them. You come into the presence
of a man whose graciousness of manner is as irre-
proachable as it is studied. There is no lack of deference in his tone or of painstaking in his bearing.
But you are straightway made sensible in a thousand
nameless ways, that you are in the presence not of a
friend, but of a critic. You are confronted not by an

open and manly confidence, but by a guarded and chilling distrust. What can you do, what good end can you hope to serve, in such company? If you are very young, your first thought will be apt to be "How very bad the world must be—nay, how wrong somehow, I must be, to be met with a demeanor which would best welcome the neighborhood of a contagious disease." And if one who is young and inexperienced encounters much of this temper of habitual distrust, what is apt to follow but the speedy development of a like temper? a temper which, in a world where in a million homes life is daily brightened by love as unselfish and faith as lofty and devotion as heroic as ever martyr dreamed, believes at last that human goodness is a vanished myth and that the falsehood of mankind is its distinguishing characteristic. O, the soured and embittered lives, that whether early or late, have fallen into that dismal distrust, and who no longer bless or brighten the world, but only embitter it with universal suspicion!

Nor is this the worst. It is a dreary thing to let go our faith in our fellowmen. It is drearier yet to lose it in ourselves. We do not realize I think, how readily distrust begets its echo in those who are distrusted. To be doubted and suspected,—this with the young is often a short road to ultimate recklessness. "What is the good of it," cries the young and sensitive nature, which has not yet learned to

appeal from the judgment of its fellows, to the verdict of its unseen Master: "What is the good of any
effort after right, if one is met at the threshold with
a sneer and a suspicion? Is there no such thing as
truth, after all? is all life hollow and false and unreal?
Well then, why should I try to be true and to hate
what is false? Why should I revere what is good,
and despise what is base and mean? No one believes
in goodness any more. It must all be a game—this
life that I am living, and cleverness, not righteousness, the aim of it." And thus is born the cynic and
the sceptic—the unbeliever in truth and the scoffer
at faith. And if there is any life more wretched and
any character more unlovable, the world has yet to
reveal it. We are wont to say that the acrid speech,
the ungenerous innuendo, the sneer of distrust with
which the lives and the speech of some persons are
daily seasoned is the fruit of their uncharitableness
or want of love. But it is not charity that is at
fault in such cases, it is faith. That thing in us
which trusts and believes, has gone barren, and it
is no wonder that, tossing feverishly upon this bed
of doubt, the very dreams that we murmur are full
of the echoes of our faithlessness.

Nor is it any wonder, either, that this faithlessness in our fellows reaches on, sooner or later, if it is
not banished and driven out, and comes to be faithlessness in God. A man who has been looking at a

landscape with a bloodshot eye, will not get rid of
it by lifting his head to look at the stars. After all,
man is the stepping-stone by which the mind climbs
to the idea of God. A child learns to love its
Saviour, by learning first to love its mother. Parenthood incarnates to its infantile mind those ideas of
a Providence, a Law and a Divine Compassion which
the person and work of Christ have incarnated to
you and me. And if it has come to pass that the
child has learned to distrust its parent, it will find
it just so much harder to believe in a good God who
has placed that parent over it. And so it is with
those of us who have done being children. The
man or woman who sees in every fellow-being some
base and mean motives as the inmost clew to their
lives will not be able to purge his vision of suspicion
when he lifts it to the Being who is above him. He
finds it far easier to distrust God just as he has distrusted man. He judges Him rather by the sterner
exceptions to the daily Providence than by its wonted
ongoing. And then, like Job, when at length he
had been ground between the cruel insinuations of
his friends, and his own darker doubts born at last
of those insinuations, he cries out, if he says any
thing at all, "God is only an unfeeling force, or a
pitiless and unrelenting destiny."

In most suggestive contrast to such a temper,
whether it illustrates itself in faithlessness concerning

our fellows or our Maker, there is a scene in the life of St. Paul which is not without eminent meaning. Near the close of his ministry, as you will remember, he writes a letter which has been preserved, to his pupil and companion, the youthful Timothy. What a ring it has, from its first word to its last, of brotherly confidence and trust! He is soon to be put to death and he knows it: he has been deserted by all but one of his fellow-laborers, and he knows that: he has made as yet but the smallest impression upon that huge mass of imperial heathenism which has bound him a prisoner in Rome; but none of these things have shaken his faith in the Master whom he serves or in that son in the ministry to whom he writes. When he called to mind, as he says, the unfeigned faith which dwelt in those who had borne and nurtured Timothy, and he adds with exquisite tenderness, "I am persuaded, is in thee, also," he had no doubt, no not for an instant, concerning this absent fellow-laborer. He was old, he was deserted, he was a prisoner, and yet what is the tone of his letter? Does he write a stinging satire upon the faithlessness of men? Does he caution Timothy against sacrificing himself to impetuous hopes, and tell him that after all zeal is well enough, but that it may better be tempered by an habitual distrust and suspicion, especially of one's fellowmen? On the contrary, were there ever words of such hopeful import,

of such serene confidence, of such tender and undi-
minished trustfulness as he speaks to this untried
young man? Now then, St. Paul was not a novice
or an innocent. He was in the largest and worthiest sense a man of the times. He knew society in
the forum and in the market-place quite as intimately
as he knew it in the temple or the synagogue. He
knew the sins of his age and his race, and the shames
and falsehoods that had stained even believing communities and Christian churches, like those of Corinth or of Ephesus. But these sad experiences had
not made of him a cynic in society nor a pessimist
in religion. He knew enough to know, how, underneath its falsehoods and unrealities, the nature that
is not true loathes its falseness and longs and aches
to be free from it. He knew that if men were to be
won to love truth and goodness, it must be by appealing to that instinct, or impulse, or aspiration in
them which could own and respond to such an appeal; and not by denying its existence. And what
he knew, he taught and preached and lived, until
that mass of corrupt and perishing heathenism to
which he went, wakened at last out of its hopeless
lethargy, owned the message of hope, and the image
of redeeming love and life which he held up before
its eyes.

For, after all, the message and the ministry of Him
to whom the apostle thus pointed that ancient faith-

lessness and despair were equally a message and a
ministry of faith in human nature. When we speak
scorningly of our kind, when we generalize hastily
from a single crime and infer the baseness of all men,
do we ever remember how utterly wanting is any
such teaching in the ministry of Christ? Read the
parable of the prodigal son, of the lost piece of
money, of one sheep that went astray. Read Christ's
encounter with Matthew, with the rich young man,
with the woman that was a sinner; do you find falling from those pure and perfect lips any thing of the
distrust, the scorn, the faithlessness in human nature
that falls too often from our most imperfect lips?
Do not mistake me. Christ's was not that charity
which thinks lightly of evil, but rather that charity which is slow to believe in it; and when He deals
with men in sin—with those whose guilt was indis-
putably clear—this, as I read it, was the supreme
thought that animated Him;—that such an one had
fallen from his real nature and could not be at peace
with himself; that there must be a better soul behind where God's long-suffering love would find a
hearing yet; and that, anyhow, through whatever
suffering and discipline, there was a possibility that
the vilest and guiltiest of those to whom He came
might be won back to truth and purity and God.

And thus it was, that coming to the race with
this inextinguishable love for the most sinful and

alienated soul, He made it possible for men to reach up and lay hold upon the salvation that He offered. When men had come to despair of themselves, suddenly they woke and found that Christ did not despair of them.

In the phraseology of science, there is what is known as a good working hypothesis. It is a probability assumed for the time to be true, as a means of reaching conclusions which lie beyond. Now, in our dealings with our fellow men which is the better working hypothesis: to assume with David in his haste, that all men are liars, or to prefer to believe that on the whole all men are not liars? Which will best serve to redeem the fallen, and steady the tempted, and inspire the timid? Give your brother man your confidence. Provoke him to love and to good works by the good which you look to see in him. And you that are fathers and mothers ennoble the child whom you are training by appealing to that which is noble in him. Amid all his faults and waywardness, strive to love him with an unextinguishable hope and trust. Believe me, what your suspicions, your scorn, your lurking distrust of him can never do, your loving confidence will far oftener and far more surely accomplish.

And so most of all in our dealings not with men, but with God. Put away from you as a cruel and monstrous perversion of His character, your thought that God does not love you, that He is watching to spy out your shortcomings, that He is a hard and inflexible task-master, measuring your performances with unpitying sternness! Such a suspicion is born, not of the truth, but of the devil. If you may trust your fellows, how much more, and more entirely, may you trust Him! Let men dispute about hell, its nature, its torments, its duration, as they will. It is a good working hypothesis that God wants to get you out of hell and to keep you out of it. Do not let your distrust of Him frustrate His bright design.

SERMON XV.

ONE ANOTHER'S BURDENS.

GALATIANS VI. 2.

" Bear ye one another's burdens, and so fulfil the law of Christ." *

A poor creature, crazed with grief and disappoint-
ment,—himself a frugal, hard-working and tenderly
devoted father, but driven to madness by a drunken
wife,—during the past week shot, first himself and
then one and the other of his children. A somewhat
coarse but keen-sighted commentator upon the dismal
tragedy remarked, on hearing of it, that the chief misfortune in the shooting seemed to be that it missed the
one person who most eminently deserved to be shot.
In other words, if there was to be any such lawless and
ghastly taking of life, it was incidentally if not chiefly,
to be deplored that the life that was taken was not
the one life that of all others seemed to be supremely
worthless. A mother without the instincts of mother-
hood, a woman who could only pass on to her children the debasing appetites which had degraded and

---

* New York, November 8, 1877.

ruined herself, surely such an one would seem to have been far less necessary to the world or to her own offspring than the virtuous, and self-respecting husband and father whom her abandoned habits drove at last to suicide and murder.

The question opens another, of still larger and farther-reaching import. We live in a world more or less marred and stained, on every hand, by vice and ignorance and crime. Indeed, so much that is painful and evil is daily brought to our notice that one dares not let his mind long rest upon it, lest he should be utterly hardened or disheartened. On the contrary, we feel it to be better that we should be busying ourselves all the time to overtake this evil and dispel this ignorance, and alleviate these effects of vice and crime. And herein, it is beginning to be charged by a certain school of thinkers whose opinions are certainly worthy of eminent respect, that we are committing the same error as the poor creature to whom I have just referred. We are, by charging ourselves with the care of the abandoned and vicious, inflicting the punishment of their wrong-doing upon ourselves, while we are allowing those who are in reality the guilty, themselves to go free. 'Look,' it is said, 'at the actual miseries of human society. From what do they chiefly come? How many of them are unavoidable miseries? How many of them are the fruit of wilful and criminal neglect? How many of them result from

wayward and most culpable self-indulgence? How
many of the diseases that fill hospitals and blight
homes and darken life, are inherited diseases, passed
on from men who ought never to have been fathers,
by women who ought never to have been mothers?
How many paupers are kept alive in almshouses to
perpetuate a pauper lineage, who, for the good of the
race, had far better, long ago, have become extinct.
We trace in nature, it is said, the working of a wise
and beneficent law which secures in all lower orders
of creation the wholesome survival of the fittest. In
the animal world, the weak, the maimed, the foolish
go to the wall, and are sooner or later extinguished
in the hardy struggle for life that goes on in the
races below us. But we, it is said, are busy, all the
time some of us, in doing all that we can to thwart
this law. 'Does it ever occur to you,' it is now and
then asked by a certain class with a good deal of per-
sistency and emphasis, 'does it ever occur to you who
are building hospitals or sustaining them, and opening
almshouses and feeding those who find shelter in
them,—that you are doing all that you can (quite innocently and unintentionally of course), to foster and
multiply the very evils to which you are ministering
a so-called relief? Take the advances of medical
science, and their application to human misery. Here
is a man who, if he were let alone, would die. Well,
he will die anyhow. The best that medical skill can

do will be to patch him up and prolong his existence for a few years—years of more or less constant weakness, suffering or weariness to himself and of burden to others, after which the inevitable end will come. But during those years such an one may become the founder of a family, and may pass on to a brood of en feebled offspring the evils and infirmities of his own temperament and constitution to be, by these, more and more widely disseminated. Would it not have been better if science had never saved such a life—so innocuous when once ended,—so harmful while prolonged? Would it not have been better, in a sense very different from that meant by the high priest Caiaphas, 'that one man should die and that a whole people should not perish?' Why should we step in between the improvident and the fruits of his improvidence? between the vicious and the bitter harvest of his vices? Why should philanthropy and Christian charity keep alive whole classes of people who had better die than live? Is religion in the world merely to get in the way of the stern but righteous laws of a Divine Providence? Is the law which, by its sure and steady working of the principle of 'natural selection' is forever ennobling all the lower orders of creation only to be thwarted when it strives to ennoble the race that is chief of all and highest? If we may not shoot, or drown, or otherwise destroy all the drunken and dissolute, or indolent or diseased or vicious, in

any community, why may we not draw a line around
them and leave them to become extinct by the self-
destroying power of their own vices, while the wise
and good devote themselves to bettering and uplifting their own kind?'

The question makes it necessary that we should
define what we mean by such terms as "ennobling,"
"bettering," "uplifting," and the like. If the object
of life is the development of human nature as a breed
of horses or fox-hounds is developed, then the principle which such objectors urge is equally sound and
wise. It is doubtful whether civilization has elevated
the physical type of man. There are athletes in
Nubia or Zanzibar whose splendid physical proportions have no equal here among us. Among such
peoples there is scant regard for the aged, the feeble,
the infirm. They drop out of the race and are trampled under foot and soon forgotten. Among such
peoples the strong is king, and the virtues which are
most esteemed among us are by them despised or else
unknown.

But what are those virtues which, outside the circumference of a Christian civilization, are thus despised or else unknown? They are virtues inculcated
by such words as these, " Ye that are strong ought to
bear the infirmities of the weak." "Now then, we
exhort you, brethren. . . . . . comfort the feeble-minded, support the weak, be patient toward all

men." "Brethren, we have been called unto liberty, only use not liberty for an occasion to the flesh, but by love serve one another." "Bear ye one another's burdens, and so fulfil the law of Christ." And words such as these we find when we come closer to them to be but echoes of other words spoken by One who began His ministry in the world by saying, "Whatsoever ye would that men should do to you, even so do to them," and who ended it by saying, "Ye call me Master and Lord; and ye say well, for so I am. If I then your Lord and Master have washed your feet" (leprous feet, impotent feet, erring and blundering feet), "ye also ought to wash one another's feet, for I have given you an example that ye should do as I have done to you." Nay, such words as I have quoted are themselves the echoes of the teaching of One who ended His life not with any mere words, but with one sublime and matchless act, in which the Perfect One gave Himself in eager sacrifice for imperfect ones, and in which there was proclaimed a law not of natural, but of supernatural, selection.

In other words, the moment that we come into the presence of the cross of Christ the world gets a new meaning and life another purpose. It is well, doubtless, that the earth should not be peopled by the thriftless, the enfeebled, the imbecile, or the vicious; and we may wisely concern ourselves more than we have hitherto done to employ every agency which does not involve cruelty or neglect that, thereby, those evils may be discountenanced, discouraged and diminished. It is by no means certain that a higher and wiser civilization ought not to, and may not give us laws which shall forbid those marriages which will inevitably perpetuate mental and physical and moral degradation or imbecility. But it is better still, that men and women should be ennobled and softened, educated and quickened by contact with such human misery as these things produce rather than be merely secluded from it. I can imagine a race in which the doctrine of the "survival of the fittest," had been deliberately enthroned as the ruling principle of its associated life. Such a race would build no orphanages, for to rear an orphanage would be to teach to its inmates that the fatherless and motherless have a claim upon the support of society; and orphans should be left to perish in order that parents might be taught the guilt of giving life to those for whom they could make no adequate posthumous provision. Such a society would build no hospitals, for hospitals are an encouragement to the maimed or enfeebled to cling to life, when they might better serve the world by surrendering life. Such a society would rear no almshouses, for if there is not work for a superfluous population, such a population has no right to exist. Above all, it would rear no churches and maintain no missions and send out no missionaries, for if the religious instinct were not strong enough in a people to provoke them to do all right things for themselves, they do not deserve that superiority which comes to nations with a reverence for, and acquaintance with religious ideas. In other words, such a society would be organized and administered upon the principle that all weakness, mental, moral or physical was to be ignored, or hustled aside, or trampled under foot. Well, I will not undertake to say what would be the ultimate outcome of such a theory of life; but this at any rate is certain, that however splendid might be the achievements of any handful of men who might survive under such a system, however magnificent their powers or gigantic their attainments might grow to be, one thing would be sure to have grown to be so gigantic, nay, so colossal, that existence in such a society would sooner or later become, even to the most favored and gifted of its inmates, utterly unendurable; and that one thing would be human selfishness: for whatever else there may be in the world that is evil or unlovely, whatever may be the vices and crimes from which we turn with intensest recoil and detestation, there is nothing on the whole, that, to any healthy human nature, is so utterly detestable as deliberate and systematic selfishness. And such a philosophy of life as I have referred to, no matter what its original motive and spring, could eventuate, ultimately, in nothing else but the deification of selfishness.

And so we are turned back to face and grapple with the evils and sorrows of life in another and very different spirit. As we look over the vast field of human suffering and misery, and see how thickly strewn it is with those maimed and bleeding forms that, like Doré's picture of the Christian martyrs in the amphitheatre, fascinate us with an equal horror and pity; as we grow impatient with the beggar who rings our door-bell and become wonted to resent his whining importunities till even our children catch the impatience of our tones and echo them in their childish speech to the poor; as we feel how wide is the ground to be covered and how scanty is the strength which we can give to it,—at such a moment, when something of an angry resentment rises in us that we are so beset and beleaguered with the halt and the maimed, the naked and the hungry, the houseless and the unemployed, we hear the voice of that wonderful servant of his Master whom no importunities provoked to impatience nor any unredeemed area of human misery however wide and dark, to hopelessness or despair,—we hear this man, I say, entreating with a tone of unmatched tenderness and love, "Bear ye one another's burdens, and so fulfil the law of Christ."

"The law of Christ." Yes, that is the whole of it. For the sum of that law is love. There lay during the past week, in an infirmary in this city, in a dark-

ened room, helpless and sightless, a man made blind
by cataract. He had crossed half a continent in the
faint hope of finding relief or cure. Beside him, when
I saw him, sat his daughter who, as I learned after-
wards, had taken up his work—a work involving long
and exposed journeys through a wild and thinly settled country on our western frontier, and who left it,
now, only to minister to this helpless and suffering
parent while he lay shrinking and quivering under
the surgeon's knife. It seemed doubtful whether the
operation would be successful, and equally doubtful
whether all this filial devotion would not be wasted
time and worthless endeavor. But, as one looked at
that woman's face of heroic sacrifice and utter self-
abnegation, one read in it how out of love's divine unselfishness there comes a sweeter and nobler fruitage
than any that could be garnered without it, even
though to-morrow, all sorrow and pain and helplessness should be swept out of the world forever.

And this consideration, as I think you will perceive, at once sets the whole subject in a light equally
lofty and clear. We may not indeed forget that while
the apostle writes, in one breath, "Bear ye one another's burdens, and so fulfil the law of Christ," he
straightway goes on to say that "every man shall
bear his own burden." We may not forget, in other
words, that while we are taught, on the one side, to
reach out a helping hand to the necessities and sor-

rows and defects of others, we are also taught on the other that we ought not, by any well-meant but ill-judged generosity of ours, to lift off from our brother's shoulders the duties and responsibilities that rightfully belong to himself. Our beneficence, in a word, must forever strive to take on such forms and to inaugurate such practical schemes, as shall not make it the nurse and feeder of that very evil which it vainly attempts to relieve. How urgent and imperious is the necessity for remembering such considerations as these, the alarming increase of pauperism in a land so young as ours is daily teaching us. The generous impulse must more than once be denied, even as we deny it to the solicitations of our own children, lest we should wrong and degrade those whom we seem to serve, by indulging it.

But when all this is said we may not forget that there are still sufferings to be alleviated and want to be relieved, and above all ignorance and hopelessness and unbelief to be enlightened and uplifted which, as Christian men and women, we dare not let alone. This church stands here, looking down upon the busy life that all the week streams past it, to and fro, and with uplifted tower and cross-capped spire tells men of a world and life that are unseen, and of consolations which no earthly fortunes or misfortunes can give or take away. But its use, even on Sundays, is hedged about with restrictions inherited from our fathers, and which some of us are not yet prepared to let go. I am not unmindful of the hospitality which is exercised here towards those who are chance-comers to these services,—a hospitality whose cheerful constancy makes me personally a debtor to those who exercise it; but, after all, we can not any of us be unaware that churches in which there are reserved rights, are not churches which are apt to be sought by those who are most in need of their ministrations. And so it came to pass that in recognition of such a want this congregation long ago built, and has lately rebuilt that free sanctuary which little more than a year ago we opened in this neighborhood and which is now the centre of so large and useful a work. To-day within the different departments of that building, will be gathered some three or four different congregations, composed now of children, and then of adults, with services at certain hours in our own mother tongue, and at others in that German language which is to so many thousands and tens of thousands of our fellow-citizens their mother tongue; and to every one of these services the access will be as free and unpurchased as the air we breathe. Into such a sanctuary, all through this Lord's day, from nine oclock in the morning until nine o'clock in the evening, any weary spirit, any sorrowing or sin-burdened heart, any man or woman or child, bereaved, lonely, perplexed or inquiring may turn for the comforting words and quickening truths of the Master's gospel and hear them, without money and without price. "I came to your church once," said a poor woman to a clergyman in a New England city, "when on my way to the wharf to drown myself. I had lost my husband, and was without friends, and my burden seemed too much for me. But I stopped at the church door—God knows what made me!—and ascended the steps. Within, I looked to see some one who should challenge me as I approached, but none did so. I found no hindrance or obstacle to my entrance and stole into the gallery while you were preaching. You spoke of a Father in heaven who will heal His children's backsliding and who loves them freely. Yes, that was the word you used, and oh, how it thrilled through my heart! I felt that that Father loved me, that He would forgive me my cowardly purpose, and, above all, that He would help me to be brave, and strong, and patient. And so it was, sir, that that open door saved me!"

Is there any one among us here who will not this morning hail it as a privilege to help to keep open such a door? The sorrows that we can not heal, the hopes that we can not rouse, shall we not rejoice that we may at any rate provide for them those divinest consolations which alone are all-sufficient. "Bear ye one another's burdens," pleads the

great Apostle, "and so fulfil the law of Christ."
Shall we not rejoice that by maintaining with our
gifts God's open house, with His free gospel, we are
thus doing our part to share our lowlier brother's burden, and better still, helping him to find his way to
One who has come to lift that burden wholly off, and
to make his humblest children free and glad forever !

SERMON XVI.

THE IMPOTENCE OF MONEY.

ACTS VIII. 18, 19, 20.

"And when Simon saw that, through laying on of the apostles' hands the Holy Ghost was given, he offered them money, saying, Give me also this power, that on whomsoever I lay hands he may receive the Holy Ghost. But Peter said unto him, Thy money perish with thee, because thou hast thought that the gift of God may be purchased with money." *

IF there is a good deal of heat in this language of St. Peter's, the provocation for it seems to have been neither slight nor small. Peter and John, in the discharge of their apostolic office, have been laying their hands upon the converts to the infant religion in Samaria, and this administration of the rite of confirmation, as we should call it, has been accompanied with those extraordinary gifts of the Holy Spirit, such as the gift of tongues, the gift of prophecy and the like, which, as we know, accompanied the ministrations of the first preachers of Christianity. Simon Magus, an astrologer, or "sorcerer," as he is called in the history, himself a baptized convert to the new faith, is a witness to these wonderful effects, and eager to be possessed of such a power himself, proposes to buy it. It is not surprising that St. Peter should have

---

* New York, May 26, 1878.

resented his proposal with indignant denunciation. This commercial conception of the gift of the Holy Spirit as a commodity for sale, or an art the secret of which could be purchased, was equally monstrous and revolting, and the double anathema of both Simon and his money, is not therefore to be wondered at.

And yet, in thus recognizing the naturalness of the apostle's language, we must not mistake the character of the man who provoked it. Simon Magus is called in the record, a sorcerer. But the word translated "sorcerer" in our English Bible has precisely the same root, and substantially the same meaning as the word translated "wise men," in the account of those who came from the east to visit the infant Saviour. In fact, the calling of a diviner was as thoroughly recognized throughout that east of which Samaria was a part, as the calling of a shepherd. Simon seems to have followed it without discredit, and equally without rebuke, for he continues it after his baptism, even as he had pursued it before; and though St. Luke describes him as "bewitching the people," the words imply no more than might be affirmed of any fanatic who, carried away by an illusion or a delusion, himself, kindled in others the same unregulated enthusiasm. Indeed, this seems to have been substantially the character of Simon, for, as later history discloses to us, his faith in his own powers was so unbounded, and his belief that he was the subject of supernatural influences was so strong, that on one occasion he declared himself able to fly, and in order to demonstrate his power, jumped from a height of the temple, and falling, fractured his thigh and both ankles; while on another, which ended his career, he insisted upon being buried alive, being confident that on the third day he should rise again. Undoubtedly, Simon Magus was one of those whose knowledge of the credulity of men, and whose experience of the pleasure which people have in the marvellous, no matter how shallow the deception that produces the marvel, encouraged and provoked him to cater to such an appetite; but that he was an utter and unscrupulous impostor is no more true than it would be to say that many excellent persons, physicians and others in our own day, who believe in the phenomena of spiritualism, are impostors.

In a word, it is not the man's general character that provokes the angry and scornful resentment of he apostle, for Simon's character was probably no better nor worse than that of the great majority of those around him. It was rather the particular proposition to buy the gifts of the Holy Ghost. And even here the offence was one chiefly of ignorance. You and I believe the Holy Spirit to be the unseen power and indwelling efficacy of the Divine Being who is our Maker and our heavenly Father. But Simon Magus had no faintest conception of the Holy Spirit, save that Peter and John possessed a gift which he had not. Whence did they get it? for what would they impart it? The throngs who sought him out were in the habit of offering him money for such arts of divination as he practiced in their behalf; and the larger and more difficult the task, the more profuse the reward. He knew how such pecuniary inducements had worked upon himself; why should they not work with equal efficacy upon these disciples of Jesus? If they had a secret, why should he not have it too? And if he was to get it, what was so sure a method of procuring what he wanted as by paying for it? And so "he offered them money, saying, Give me this power, that on whomsoever I lay hands he may receive the Holy Ghost."

I do not know that the age in which Simon lived was especially a commercial age; but whether Jew or Samaritan, Simon himself was a child of Israel, of that race which has always been a buyer when it could not be a seller, and which in one generation bought a brother's birthright for a mess of pottage, even as in another it sold its Saviour for thirty pieces of silver. And thus, in Samaria, and with Simon, the proposition was equally natural and characteristic.

It would be scarcely less so, I think, if Simon were living to-day. Whatever may have been the distinctive peculiarity of Simon's age and generation, there can not be much doubt about ours. There have been, in the history of the world, successive ages, each of a characteristic type, as, *e. g.*, the age of the shepherds, illustrated in the long centuries of pastoral life in the East; the age of conquest, as depicted in the story of the Persian kings; the age of the arts and of letters, as seen in Greece; the age of civic rule and military despotism, as revealed in the history of Rome; the age of religious enthusiasm, as traceable in the history of the middle ages and the crusades; the age of luxury, as found in the France of the Louises, and of revolution, as found in the France of the Bonapartes. And as all these various ages have been marked by their distinctive characteristics so is ours. In one of these ages men worshipped military superiority; in another, culture; in another, heroism; in another, self-indulgence. But, though in all of them men recognized the uses of wealth, and sought it by cleverness or by force, in no one among them all did the conception of the capabilities of wealth come to be so fevered and exaggerated as in our own. We are living in times when men not merely believe that wealth is of all other things the one thing most desirable (men have believed that, all the way from the time of the rich young man whom Christ sent away "exceeding sorrowful," on to this hour), but when they believe also that there is nothing that is greatly worth having that can not be purchased with money.

And therefore it is that this answer of Peter to the proposal of Simon is so eminently timely and pertinent: "Thy money perish with thee, because thou hast thought that the gift of God may be purchased with money." This power that you covet, is a communicable power, but you can not buy it! You have seen these common-place people upon whom apostolic hands have been laid, somehow quickened by them into a disclosure of powers such as your poor arts have never dreamed of; but all the money that you could marshal, if the wealth of an empire were at your command, could not purchase the least or lowliest of those powers!

"Well, what of it?" one saturated with the spirit of our time might easily answer. "I mean no disrespect to religion, and I imply no want of faith in the gifts and powers of what you call the Holy Spirit, when I admit, frankly, that they are not the gifts and powers that I crave. But there are other things that I do crave, and those things are the things which can be purchased with money. I look about me in the world and see, as I read its social and political and even its domestic phenomena, that there is nothing so potent as wealth. I find that in the society in which I move, nothing covers so many faults or transmutes, if not into virtues, then into innocent foibles, so many vices, as money. I find that neither the joy of birth nor the tragedy of death are usually

separate from the questions, 'What will he inherit?'
or 'What did he leave?' I find that while we scorn
the French marriage of convenience in name, we hallow and observe it most religiously in fact. I find
that poverty, if not a disgrace, is somehow accounted
an impertinence, and that the vulgarities of ostenta-
tious display are pardonable and even admirable in
precise proportion to the dimensions of the fortune
that indulges in them. I find, above all, that every
taste that I cultivate makes wealth more desirable
and poverty more irksome. I find that while I can
acquire the habits of luxurious living with facility, I
can surrender them only with pain. And finally, I
find, that, no matter how selfish or unscrupulous,
how hard and imperious has been my career while
living, it is only necessary that, in the matter of the
accumulation of money it shall have been an exceptionally successful career to secure for me, when
dying, the applause of mankind. Wherein then, consists the folly or even the error, so long as I frankly
own that I do not care for the gifts and graces of the
Holy Spirit, in my owning also that every thing else
that I do care for can be purchased with money?"

That error and that folly consist, I venture to
reply, in this: that these gifts of the Spirit which
Simon would fain have bought with money, are after
all but the type and emblem of every other best
gift in all the world, and that of these as of those,

it is everlastingly and inflexibly true that they are not for sale. Recall some of them for a moment, and see if it is not so.

(*a*) Many of us here, for instance, have drifted, in some experience, of travel into one of those European refuges of the invalid like Ems or Karlsbad. They are places where people whose lungs or limbs or livers are diseased have come together to drink the waters and submit to the regimen, or be washed whole again in the baths. What an assemblage of halt and lame and diseased it is! O those melancholy processions of gloomy-visaged and despondent men and women! Who that has ever seen them can forget them? I have heard of one from among them who, while resting in some little inn among the hills, burst into a storm of passionate denunciation because a ruddy and healthy-looking servant had entered his apartment. How dared such an one, whose bounding step and glowing color were a mockery of his sufferings insult him with the offensive contrast of her unwelcome presence! And yet the peasant girl was only a peasant, and the dyspeptic and jaundiced invalid was a prince and a millionnaire. Would he not have been willing, think you, to have shared his millions if he could have bought with them the other's single gift of health, the keen thrill of pleasure, the bounding sense of the beauty and loveliness of nature; in one word, the mere joy of living? Unfortunately, however, for persons of large fortunes and impaired livers, none of these things are for sale.

(*b*) Again, next in rank to the unpurchasable boon of health, is that higher boon of mental culture. There are very few really healthy people in the world, and there are hundreds of thousands of men and especially of women, all over the land, who rarely know a day and never a week without an experience of pain. And yet they are possessors of a secret which makes them habitually insensible to pain. There are accomplishments, more or less simple, as the case may be, in which they can so lose themselves that, for the time, at any rate, nothing harmful or unwelcome really touches them; and above all, in the pages of a book, whether poem, or history, or tale, or essay, it matters not, they can so pass out of the consciousness of their outer world into the consciousness of that other and inner world to which the poet, the dramatist or the historian has introduced them, that penury and loneliness and pain will be for the time being equally and utterly forgotten.

But such a pleasure as this is not a purchasable pleasure. Money can not even buy accomplishments, much less that finer culture of the mind which comes only with the habit of mental discipline and the subtler pleasure of thinking. Indeed, just because high living is usually so fatal to high thinking, the pleasures of culture are almost prohibited to the merely rich. They come to live so largely in an atmosphere of display, their daily habits are so fatal to repose and consecutiveness of occupation, their intimates are so almost invariably people of feeble intellectual furnishing, that it follows inevitably that the mind becomes at once sluggish and frivolous. Now then, it does not matter that such persons have never known (because incapable of knowing) the joys of high intellectual activity and so can not greatly miss what they have never tasted. What they do know is that weariness of *ennui*, that restlessness of interest, that impatient querulousness in the midst of their surroundings, that proneness to idle gossip, to perilous intrigue, to coarser indulgence which is the everlasting tendency of an unoccupied and habitually luxurious life. So thoroughly is this understood in countries where wealth is hereditary that its inheritors are wont, often, to create occupations as a defence against the dangers of their peculiar circumstances. But when such occupations are wanting, the intellectual apathy is at times a hideous and appalling nightmare, and the untrained mind would often gladly buy the joys that others find in pleasures that are purely mental. But, here as before, such pleasures are not for sale.

(*c*) Much more, and more tragically is this true,

when we pass from the domain of the intellect to that of the affections. Love is not for sale; and that mysterious sentiment which must be won and deserved—not purchased, never goes along with a jointure nor can be made over with transfers of real estate. So long as the world lives, I suppose, men and women will sell themselves, and other men and women will sell their children. And how hard some of these last will try to put their hearts into the transaction and so ennoble a bargain with an emotion! Nevertheless, it can not be done. Wayward, capricious, unreasoning as are, too often, those strong and tenacious attachments which survive neglect and outlive betrayal, no one ever knew one such in all the world that was won by money. There have been plenty of people with no capacity for such an affection who have bartered themselves for some one else's possessions, but in selling their persons or their accomplishments they have usually sold all that they had to sell. The power of greatly and unselfishly loving another was not in them, and what they had not to deliver they could not sell. But, where in any man or woman there has been such a capacity, the heart has steadily and invariably refused to follow the beckoning of mere worldly possessions. If any one else loves us, we may be sure that it is not for what we have, but for what we are.

(*d*) And that reminds me of one other unpurchasable possession, which I may venture to mention this morning. I mean what we call sometimes indifferently "a good conscience," or peace of mind. The world has always had in it a great many people who, having lived selfish and grasping lives, have striven, before they were done with life, to square accounts by the lavish distribution of their means. All along, as they have toiled and schemed and hoarded, they have been uncomfortably conscious of the compassion of some of those who were about them. There have been thoughtful men, and quiet women, who have looked at them with a strange sadness in their eyes, and with an undertone of sorrowful tenderness in their speech. And when they have encountered such persons they have been dimly sensible that these quiet neighbors of theirs had a secret of peace, of contentment, above all of hopeful and certain anticipation, of which they themselves knew nothing. O, what would they not give if they could buy that! They hear other men talk as though departing out of this life were simply going out of one room into another where a dear friend whom we have long known is waiting to welcome us, and as they look forward into the downward-opening vista that seems so dark they would give every thing that they are worth if they could buy a serenity like that. Nay, more, as they look backward—as they remember—what else would they not give if they but had it to give, if somehow they could transform those cruel and accusing memories. In one word, if an undaunted and joyful faith and a serene and blameless conscience could be bought, oh, how eagerly they would buy them! But that peace of God which passeth all understanding, passeth all price as well!

I want to say one word, if it be no more, to reach the hearts of those here who are young. You are living, my young brother and sister, in an atmosphere, where the loudest bid that is made is the bid for money. Almost every thing that you see and hear, the people you meet, the amusements you share, too much, I fear, of the literature that you read, idolizes and idealizes the power of money. Be afraid, I entreat you, of an idolatry so poor and mean! Money, in itself considered, is neither good nor bad. It is an instrument, an agency, a weapon. You may have it without being bad and you may be without it without being good. But oh, to live for it as an end, to bend all your energies to its acquirement, to fret and scold and repine because you are without it, this, believe me, is the death of all nobleness and the doom of aspiration. There must have been some hours in your life when your heart has thrilled with a genuine aspiration, and when, sitting alone in the stillness of your room, you have poured over the page that has told you of the great names that have made humanity immortal,—men and women who have carried its sorrows and its hopes upon their hearts,—who have illumined its low places with the beauty of their lives, and who, as they moved onward and upward printing their footsteps in blood on the stony steeps have left behind them the lustre of a nobility that can never pale and have filled the busy air throug'ı which they passed with the fragrance of a heroism' that can never die. And at such moments,—when all the house has been hushed in its midnight stillness and you have dropped your book, feeling your nature all aglow with the great thoughts that have been kindled within you, — surely, then, you have longed to be like those nobler beings and to follow their radiant footsteps. Cling to that longing, my young brother,—cling to it, and follow it as well, for, sooner or later, this love of goodness, this reverence for nobleness, this aspiration after unselfishness, will bring you into the presence of One who is the best, the divinest, the most unselfish of all.

And yet, how poor He was! I wonder that it has not oftener occurred to us to think how utterly and absolutely Christ triumphed without the aid of money. Nowadays there is no enterprise, however unworldly its aims, that must not rest upon a pecuniary basis. And yet there has lived in the world one Being, who from first to last was absolutely and utterly penniless. Since He came and went away, what colossal fortunes have been heaped up, what imperial wealth has been ravished from conquered peoples and hoarded in the palaces of kings, what mighty combinations of capital have ruled the credit of the civilized world and made even princes and sovereigns to fawn obsequiously upon their possessors. What has become of them? Who remembers them?

But all the while the sway of that Galilean peasant who when He was in the world had not where to lay His head, broadens and deepens and advances. Would you possess the secret of His resistless spell? Verily, if like Simon you come to buy it with mere money, you and your money shall most surely perish together. But if you come discerning that the gifts of God are gifts which money can not purchase, then indeed you may hope to learn that secret which transfigures life and death alike, which fills the heart with the sunshine of an immortal hope, and which, thus, shall make you rich forever!

SERMON XVII.

THE CHRISTIAN LIFE ORGANIC.

ACTS I. 15, 16, 22.

"And in those days Peter stood up in the midst of the disciples and said . . . . . . Men and brethren . . . . . . of these men which have companied with us all the time that the Lord Jesus went in and out among us . . . . . . must one be ordained to be a witness with us of His resurrection." *

THE suicide of Judas Iscariot on Good Friday, created a vacancy in the number of the twelve apostles. During the forty days of His earthly ministry which followed His resurrection, Christ, while speaking to His disciples of many other things "concerning the kingdom of God," does not seem to have spoken or acted concerning this. In other words, He leaves this vacancy in the number of those twelve whom He Himself had originally chosen to be filled by those twelve themselves, together with those others, as we are told "about an hundred and twenty," who made up, on those earliest days of its existence, the sum total of the membership of the Christian Church.

And this is the duty to which, in the words which I have just read to you, the Apostle Peter summons them. How characteristic of Peter it was! The lit-

---

* New York, May 25, 1879.

tle handful of Christian believers who had just seen
their risen Lord and Master vanish in the clouds were
waiting for—they scarcely knew what. He who had
bidden them wait, had called it "the promise of the
Father," "the gift of the Comforter," the "Spirit
of truth," "the baptism of the Holy Ghost," and
though, as yet, they could only dimly guess what
those words stood for, they knew at least that they
stood for that for which the world had long been
waiting, "light—more light and clearer." I wonder
it did not just here occur to some of Peter's calmer
and less impetuous companions to ask themselves
whether, before choosing a new apostle, Peter and
the rest of them had not better wait for the gift that
would so soon make them so much more competent
to choose? I wonder if some more phlegmatic disciple in the infant church did not whisper to his companion, "How hasty our brother Peter always is!"
It would not have been surprising if it had seemed so.
Christ's farewell words to His disciples say nothing
of any duty which belonged to them between His
ascension and the day of Pentecost but this, "Depart
not from Jerusalem, but wait for the promise of the
Father." It was a call not to activity, but to stillness
and expectancy. But Peter at once organizes a council and proceeds to an Episcopal election.

And, unquestionably, Peter was right. The choice
of Matthias in the place of the traitor Judas, was at-

tended with every immediate and subsequent evidence that God had designed and approved it. The day of Pentecost when it came, brought to Matthias equal gifts of grace and wisdom and power with the others, and made his subsequent ministry a track of glory for the cross and of triumph for the truth. It is very true that Christ had given to the eleven apostles no command to fill up their ranks to their original number, nor to do a great many other things, which nevertheless, they did. But it is none the less true that, if they were not acting according to the letter of His commands, they were acting according to the spirit of them. His Church was a building. He Himself had laid the foundations. They were to rear the superstructure. And so St. Peter himself calls the Christians of Pontus, Galatia and Bithynia " living stones, built up into a spiritual house." But by whom? Plainly by men who, like Matthias, had been called and commissioned and consecrated not by Christ Himself, but by His apostles. In a word, these men recognized it to be their first duty after their Lord's ascension to fill up the ranks and perfect the organization, and so enlarge the influence and increase the working power of that divine agency which Christ had committed to their charge.

What now, was that divine agency? By some we are told that it was the truth which Christ preached; and according to the differing sympathies of those who say this, that truth is made out to be the truth taught in the Sermon on the Mount, or that other truth taught in the sacrifice on Calvary, and re-affirmed in St. Paul's epistle to the Romans. In other words it is the morality of the New Testament as interpreted by the Liberalist, or the dogma of the New Testament as interpreted by the Calvinist. To both these schools of thought Christ did not so much found a church as He did inculcate a philosophy, and both of them in turn have been almost supplanted by a third school of which still more is heard in our day and which affirms that Christ did not come so much to proclaim a truth or affirm a dogma as He did to live a life. The power of His gospel is the power of His life. The spell of His ministry is the spell of His person. What is wanted is to see that, to feel its beauty, to be fired by its nobleness, to be inspired by its spirit. And if only that can be attained, organization, what men call the church, is of small account. One church is as good as another, if not better. Indeed, the question whether Christ organized a church, whether He instituted sacraments and initiated men into a visible fellowship,—all this is of such extremely small consequence that it is, practically, of no consequence at all.

Whether this be so or not, you who are at home in this holy house will bear me witness that I have not unduly insisted here upon the divine origin or the divine authority of the church. In looking over a record of more than a thousand sermons which I have preached from this pulpit, I have not found it easy to find many of them which relate to this subject. But meantime, in pulpits without number, and in places almost as numerous where there are no pulpits, we have heard the doctrine proclaimed in connection with all sorts of worship, and with no worship at all, that "organization is not life," and that Christendom having already spent too much of its time in worshipping the drag and the net, needs to turn its back upon machinery, to let go its faith in organization and to follow truth, no matter how formless may be its creed, nor how heterogeneous its fellowship.

Let us admit freely that organization is not life, but when we do so, let us understand that without organization there can be no life. In nature we know of life at all, only as it exhibits itself under organized forms, and precisely as life in an individual, physical, muscular, nervous, sentient must be organized life, even so St. Paul affirms must the life of divine truth in the world, be an organized life with a head, and hands and feet—in other words with that which governs and that which communicates and that which obeys.

We have lately witnessed in New York the conclusion of a most interesting and instructive effort to ignore that truth. The other Sunday morning (selected not at all because it was Sunday morning, but because its enforced leisure suited the convenience of a number of cultivated people) an accomplished gentleman whom I will not call a clergyman, because no one probably would disclaim the title with more decided emphasis than himself, disbanded the congregation to which he had been ministering for more than twenty years, closed the doors of the hall in which he and they had been wont to assemble, and departed to foreign lands. This gentleman had brought to his work as a leader and teacher—if indeed his rare modesty would have allowed him even so much titular authority as those two words imply—the most thorough culture, exceptional intellectual endowments, and a manly and generous spirit. If he did not hold truths which to you and me are supremely precious, he did not so far as I know speak of them with needless contempt or ridicule. His life before this community has been one of singular elevation and purity, and of the most stainless and unselfish integrity. It was my privilege to know him, and I never met him without being impressed by the modesty, the gentleness, and the dignity of his bearing, and by the kindly and generous quality of his sympathies.

With the added weight of such gifts and such a character, this accomplished apostle of the most advanced liberalism, taught and labored in New York for nearly a quarter of a century. His "society" or association of listeners, was not a church, and his worship was without a creed. A half a dozen volumes found as conspicuous and frequent a place in his Sunday exercises, as did the Bible, and the word of Gautama was quite as sacred as the word of Christ. Nobody was ever baptized, for there was no organized fellowship to be baptized into, nor any sacred Name to be baptized by. No Sacrament of the Holy Communion was ever celebrated, for both the symbols and the sacrifice which they commemorated were to this "society" equally meaningless and superannuated. No Good Friday solemnity nor Christmas nor Easter joy was ever called to mind there, for the facts which to us those days so vividly recall were equally and utterly rejected. The Son of God was not born of Mary nor did He die for our sins nor rise again for our justification.

Now then, that such a teaching as this was persisted in for more than twenty years without greatly impressing the community to whom it was addressed, does not prove that it was false. If it did, then the unsuccessful efforts of Christian missionaries to convert Mohammedans, would prove that Christianity is false, which the Moslem undoubtedly and thoroughly believes. But the failure of such an effort, so long continued, under such exceptionally favorable auspices, with such marked and distinguished ability, does prove that in the domain of religion, there can not be life and growth and perpetuity without that thing which we call organization, and therefore that in perfecting the organization of the infant church, the apostles and brethren who did so were walking equally in the path of duty and the path of wisdom. When a farmer in the Salt Lake Valley constructs that clever and ingenious system of sinuous and interlacing tile water-courses by which the melting snows of the Wausatch Mountains are conducted to every remotest corner of his vineyards and cornfields, he has not thereby secured the smallest guarantee that the snow will fall, or that it will melt, or that it will obey the law of gravitation and run down hill into his tanks, any more than up hill into Lake Tahoe. These things are ordered by God not by him, and his orchards blossom and his corn sprouts, not because he has laid so many feet of tile drain-pipe, but because God has put into the melted snow or the chance shower some mysterious power of making that arid desert of sand with its silex and potash to burst forth, straightway so soon as the water has touched it, and bud and blossom as a rose. But none the less, as things are, that arid and desert valley would never have burst into flower if the farmer's simple machinery had not so organized and utilized these forces of nature that the baptism of the one became the new birth and resurrection of the other.

And this, at any rate, is the lesson of such a parable, as it is of all history for you and me. The

Church of God is in the world, not as a human invention, but as a divine appointment to be applied by human hands. Its fellowship is not salvation, but it is a means of salvation. Its sacraments are not grace, but they are channels of grace. Its Bible is not a charm or a talisman, but it is a teacher and guide. Its services are not spells, but they are helps and refreshments. Its fellowship is not an order of infallibility, but it is the "fellowship of the saints." It may often be that we have joined in its services, and knelt at its altar, and risen and gone away, as cold and unmoved as we came. It may be that we have listened to the words of yonder Bible, or caught dreamily the cadence of some prayer or hymn, with a conscious sense how unreal and empty the whole order of devotions was to our own hearts. But if there have been other moments when something has touched and stirred us, if ever the pierced hands of One who once suffered in our stead have seemed to be held out to us, and if, to the question, "What are these wounds in thine hands?" there has broken upon our startled ears the answer, "These are they with which I was wounded in the house of my friends"—that mingled sob of penitence, of self-accusation, of devotion which those words perhaps awakened in us, was not kindled by the teachings of the lyceum nor the banter of the assembly. It was the Church of God and the voice of the Spirit of God echoing and re-echoing through her services, that stirred that forgotten hunger, and thrilled you with penitence and with praise.

And therefore let us own, that the example of that little company in the upper room in Jerusalem may wisely find imitators here and among us. There is an incident in the life of Christ which bears upon this subject and which has not always been recognized, in its largest and deepest meaning. It occurs just after Jesus has emerged from the descent and baptism of the Spirit and from His struggle in the desert. That baptism and that struggle marked, with Him, the ending of the old life and the beginning of the new. Behind Him were the boyhood and youth of preparation, before Him was the struggle and sacrifice of work. And now, at last, lifted into the full power of the Spirit and conscious of the august calling that was upon Him, whither and toward what does He turn ? We open the pages of St. Luke's Gospel and we read, " And He came to Nazareth, where He had been brought up; and as His custom was, He went into the synagogue on the Sabbath-day and stood up to read." What ! had He not risen above that ? could the dull preachings and the drawling prayers say any thing to Him ? What charm could He longer feel in these childish Sabbath usages, the decent dress, the restful hours, the flowing together of families, and the walking to the house of God in company ? Did not

He, above all, live in a constant air of divine communion, and mingle with the eternity where all is consecrated alike? Do what He might, go where He
would, walking early on the beach, sitting by the well
at noon, or kneeling by night upon the mountain
grass, jostled by the city multitudes, or borne upon
the sea alone, was He not always with the Father—
Himself a better sanctuary than He could ever find?
"What could a nature at that height," some one has
asked,* "have to do with any sacred enclosure of time
or space? And yet at Nazareth, where He had been
brought up, He went as His custom was, into the synagogue on the Sabbath day. To nothing newer or
higher does He turn, but to the village sanctuary, on
the stated day of rest, to the place and on the day
that had been sacred to the fathers before Him. In
other words, the first thing which under freshest inspiration Christ did, was to resume the dear old ways,
to fall in with the well-known season, to unroll the
same venerable page, only to find a new meaning in
words that had long carried their rhythm to His
heart."

May we not wisely believe that what was His custom may healthfully be ours, no less? You will have
been very fortunate if you have not more than once
met those self-reliant persons who, as they tell you,

---

* Martineau, "Tides of the Spirit," p. 3–4.

feel themselves above the superstition of prayer. Their busy or gay and crowded days and evenings leave them no chance to realize a world outside that world which can be seen and heard and handled. They are conscious of no relation to an unseen Lord and an unseen life, and they can not see why they should pretend to be. Religion, the Church, the Lord's day and the Lord's house—these are things for the nursery and the schoolroom, a discipline or else a resource, for the ignorant and the feeble-minded. For themselves they have long ago outgrown them, and can only condescendingly compassionate those who have not.

And yet, it was Christ, after all, who was right, and not any of these. Theirs is the fleeting humor of the hour, the fashion of a judgment that passeth away; as most surely His custom was witness to a want that endures. When He stood there in the synagogue, He was in the current of the deepest, mightiest and most enduring tide of human sentiment and conviction, that conviction which sooner or later forces itself home upon every human soul: that it wants God, that it must seek Him and must find Him, and that if anywhere on earth, there are currents of His life, audible voicings of His love, visible boundaries of His fellowship, actual and tangible symbols and sacraments of His grace, it wants these no less! I honor with my whole soul that protest against the formalism of the Church, which, whether in other ages or in our own, resents the tendency to make of these things the whole of religion—a protest of which so much of the religious teachings of our day has had so much to say. I honor no less that vehement and robust indignation which denounces the temper that hands over all men who do not belong to your Church or mine or some other of equal historic pretensions, to the uncovenanted mercies of God. I believe with all my heart that a Baptist and Methodist and a Presbyterian can be saved as well as a Churchman, and that in individual cases any one of these may happen to have lived saintlier lives than some of their Churchlier brethren. Nay, more, I believe, with equal earnestness and sincerity, what a good many of my evangelical brethren may not be so ready to concur in, that a Unitarian and a Universalist and a Roman Catholic can be saved as well as a Churchman, and that there have been, and doubtless are saints in every one of these communions at whose feet many of us might wisely sit. But all this does not affect in the smallest degree, the question whether or no Christ has founded a Church, whether or no you and I have sought, and as we believe, found its fellowship; or whether having found that fellowship, we are not bound to walk in it, to work in it, to live in it, and to die in it. All this is not in the smallest degree affected by the question, what other fellowships, brotherhoods, associations there may be outside of it, or how numerous or how pious or cultivated or how wealthy these may be. All these questions are questions of statistics, or perhaps of a certain social or historical or political significance, if you choose. But to erect them into any thing more; and, on the other hand, to reduce the duty of having one's place in that organic fellowship which is of divine institution and of apostolic ordering, to a mere matter of taste or fancy or inclination, in which every most recent vagary is as true as any most ancient and scriptural principle is possibly false; this is not charity nor liberality nor toleration, nor any thing else that is manly or noble or generous, but the merest chatter of a maudlin sentimentalism.

In other words, the Church exists in the world not to enjoy our patronage, to invite our criticism, to gratify our taste, but to accept our discipleship. Her organized life, the due succession of her ministry, the due ministration of her sacraments, the stated order of her worship, the ceaseless proclamation of her Lord's message,—all these things are not less important, less essential to-day, than when in the beginning Peter convened the hundred and twenty disciples to choose the apostle Matthias. This Christian organization is divine, and as such it speaks its message and holds forth its ministrations. It may be that some of us have been taught another and very inferior view of this whole subject. It may be that, consciously or unconsciously, we have come to regard the Church as a kind of social appendage, a rather more dignified marrying and burying and baptizing association, which we are to make use of when tradition or custom or decorum constrains us to, and at other times conveniently forget. But if indeed the Church be no more than that, surely it would be more manly and more truthful to draw out from it and stand aloof from it, altogether. For the moment that we look into the history of its origin, and the charter of its claims, we find that its own position is an utterly and radically different one. It asserts of itself nothing less than a divine origin, and it demands a definite obedience. We are to do certain things, to submit to certain ordinances, to observe certain days and rules and usages because there is claimed for them a heavenly authority. We may say that that authority is groundless, but until we have proved it, our allegiance is not an option, it is a debt.

And that truth, I take it, there is much need to master for ourselves, and to inculcate among our children. More and more there is growing up a disposition among parents to permit all matters of religious observance to be with their offspring mere matters of choice or preference. Your child must learn French and German and drawing; but he shall learn his catechism and his Bible lesson and a reverent observance of this holy day, if he chooses, and not otherwise. A more dismal and irrational folly it is not easy to conceive of! I do not say that there may not have been folly in another and opposite direction. I am not unmindful that religious teaching has been sometimes made a dreary and intolerable burden. But surely we can correct one excess (not I apprehend very frequent or very harmful) without straightway flying to an opposite and worse one.

And so I plead with you who are parents to train your children in ways of reverent familiarity with God's word, God's house, and God's day. Let them understand that something higher than your taste or preference makes these things sacred and binding, and constrains you to imbue them with their spirit. And that you may do this the more effectually, give them, I entreat you, that mightiest teaching which consists in your own consistent and devout example. We are nearing a season when many of us will be widely scattered. Some of you are soon going to other lands and to countries and capitals beyond the sea. You have asked us to pray for you, thus acknowledging that you need God's care off the coast of Ireland, quite as really as in the streets and homes of New York. Remember, I beseech you, what that request of yours implies. Remember that God sees you as plainly in London as in Washington. Be ashamed to do in Paris what you would be ashamed to do in New York. When Sunday comes there, remember that it has not ceased to be Sunday, because you can not hear your own church bells and kneel in your own pew. Wherever you go, you are a baptized member of the Church, and treachery to your baptismal vow is as disloyal under a foreign flag as it would be under your own.

And all this applies with equal emphasis to those of us who stay at home. We will almost all of us find ourselves at some time or other during the summer among strange surroundings. Let us not mistake our obligations. Whether in the mountains, or by the sea-shore, or in the woods, we shall not have outrun our duty to God any more than our duty to our neighbor. Let us not be ashamed to own it. If you are near to a church of your own communion, see to it that you are found there on the Lord's day. If there is any struggling servant of the Master striving in some of the waste places in the wilderness to build up the spiritual temple of the Lord, let him not be disco raged by your ridicule or your indifference. Help the village choir and the village pastor and the village flock, by your manly and womanly sympathy and encouragement and substance. Stand by the church of your affections and the faith of your fathers, wherever you may go. And if it is true, to-day, that you have never yet adequately learned to prize the one or to hold to the other, come and stand with those who gathered in that upper room, on that first Sunday after Ascension Day, and with them wait, and listen, and look up. To them, thus waiting, there came the rushing, mighty wind, the cloven fiery tongues, the baptism of the Spirit. And to you, expecting this, that kindling flame, that quickening breath, that new life of the Spirit, is as near and as transforming now, as then!

SERMON XVIII.

THE EMPTY LIFE.

ST. MATTHEW XII. 44.

"Then he saith, I will return unto my house from whence I came out: and when he is come, he findeth it empty, swept and garnished." *

I SHALL take these words, somewhat apart from their connection, though, as I believe, in exactest accord with their spirit.

That connection you will doubtless remember. The whole passage, as Christ originally spoke it, is a portrait or history of the power of evil in a man—how, sometimes, it is exorcised for a time; how it returns often to its old abode in the heart in which it had reigned; how, alas, almost as often, it finds that heart empty and untenanted by any better inmate, and how, seizing the opportunity which is afforded to it by such emptiness, it leads back with it seven other spirits worse and wickeder even than itself, and so makes the end of the wretched being whom it thus possesses immeasurably darker and drearier than his beginning.

Certainly, the parable, if parable we may call it,

---

* New York, October 8, 1876.

is a very expressive portraiture of a large part of human history. This struggle of the soul with evil, this grappling of a man with his own bad habits, the partial conquest, the temporary banishment of some base custom, the newly-gained freedom from some malign inspiration, some weak and wicked motive that has ruled him, and then, the surging back into the empty soul of the powers that, lately driven out, had so long held it captive, the greater impetus with which, when a degrading habit or a mean motive thus returns upon us, if it is suffered to return at all, it hurries the soul onward and downward,—all this is something with which no one of us who has faced the graver experiences of life can be long or largely unfamiliar.

And it is in the line of such an experience, that I propose to speak to-day, though from a standpoint somewhat more local and particular. That standpoint is suggested by what may almost be called one of the social habits of our American people—certainly of a great many of our city congregations. I refer to the habit of migration,—that habit, which, with the growth among us, of wealth, of artificial forms of life, of constant and worrying strain, whether in the office or in the home, is annually increasing among us, of breaking up our accustomed modes of living and of exchanging them for a time for others, usually simpler, less engaged, and more rural. In other words, while it is true that there are whole classes of people in a great city who never leave it unless it be for a day at a time, it is also true that there is a large and annually increasing class who abandon the city every summer and return to it every autumn, and, in doing so, make a break more or less abrupt in their wonted employments, interests, and recreations, so that when they return to take up, as many of them are now doing, the thread of their city life, they find themselves much in that condition which is so expressively described in the text. The house is "empty, swept, and garnished." The life is free, unoccupied, and disengaged. "Things have n't begun," we say. People have not, or have not all, come back to their wonted haunts. The social machinery which, a few weeks or months later, will have caught so many lives up into its huge whirl and clatter, has not yet commenced to revolve. We know, many of us, very well, that if we can be content to wait, excitement, occupation, what we call, with such a sad because such an unconscious sarcasm, "being busy," will come fast enough; we know that other idle people, with perhaps more energy or ingenuity than belongs to us, will be scheming and planning to stir the sluggish pulses of our social life until the surface of that life shall be whitened with the wonted froth of evening and morning and mid-day excitements, each crowding upon the other with incessant and exhausting frequency; and we know, too, that however much we may affect to be indifferent to such excitements, nothing is easier than to drift with a current which sets strongly and runs swiftly in one common tendency towards them.

But now, the current is not in motion. The social world as we are wont to call it, has not as yet re-organized itself. There is pause, repose, unusual and for some of us almost embarrassing leisure. Our evenings are little interrupted. The door-bell, whose dread clang will strike terror a little later into so many tired brains, has scarce begun to ring, and we find ourselves half surprised that the house is so still and the day so little intruded upon.

And thus there comes to us one of those occasions in life, which occur oftener than we are wont to recognize, perhaps, but which are yet far enough apart to indicate their character and purpose. As the mind pauses at such a point it realizes that in a certain sense the shaping of its destiny, the direction of its interests and occupations, and so the quality of its aspiration, is given back into its keeping. If it has been drifting along, hitherto, yielding itself up to be influenced by the chance motives and impulses which come with the day, here is an opportunity to give one's days a definite direction and one's life a fresh bent and aim, and to do it with decision and emphasis. If one has been spending a gay or idle or somewhat purposeless summer, and is very likely, unless otherwise resolutely determined, to spend an equally gay or idle or purposeless winter, here is such a chance as comes but once in any year, and not, it maybe, to all of us even as often as that, to come up upon the ground of this resolute purpose, and to say clearly and commandingly to one's self, "I have been drifting long enough. Now I intend, by the grace of God, to begin living and acting. Life to me shall henceforth have an honest meaning and a consistent purpose. I may not be able to realize even my own poor ideal; but I will have an ideal and I will keep it before me. If hitherto I have been a waif—a very feather caught by every passing wind and blown as chance might dictate—I will, from this time at any rate, resolve to give to my life a definite ordering, to busy myself with some sort of earnest and wholesome endeavor either for the well-being of other people or my own. This I will do, God helping me, and do it with my whole heart!"

In other words, such a season as this is one which presents anew to a great many persons among us the question, "What do you mean to do with your own life? Do you mean that it shall have any serious, earnest, really robust and righteous purpose at all? or do you mean to go on leaving it to be shaped and colored and filled out just as any chance hand may choose to mix the colors and lay them on? You have known what it was to be the creature of outside impulses which, when the week or month or year was done have left you to look back and own that though you were so much older and ought to have been so much wiser than before, there was nothing whatsoever to show for that time either of learning or achievement. You have known what it was to get up in the morning saying, " Here is another day. Let me stop and think what are the means which social usage, the vanity, ambition or prodigality of somebody else has provided for my killing it." Nay, you have even known what it was to cram the day so full of excitement and movement and gaiety, that when at length you were alone at night, and had put off the cumbrous artificialities of an attire which is so apt a symbol of the artificial sphere of its display, you felicitated yourself that you had not even an instant in which, to use your own unconsciously expressive phrase, you "could stop and think." Well now, have you ever thought of the drift and tendency of such a life as that? how, sooner or later, the mere excitement of the mind, of the imagination, of the senses, comes to be the end and aim of existence itself, until at length nothing that is sacred or precious is allowed to stand in the way of the gratification of that excitement?

I know it may be objected at this point that there is very little need of such a warning as this, even as there is but a very small class to whom it may properly be addressed. I know, in other words, that it may be urged that there are very few people in a land like ours who have nothing to do, or whose occupations and interest are not pretty definitely marked out for them. But on the other hand it certainly can not be denied that such an element in our social life as a largely unoccupied class is rapidly growing among us. As wealth increases, as we multiply men-servants and maid-servants in our houses, as life becomes less primitive and more artificial, there come to be found a large number of persons, both men and women, who have little or nothing to do, unless they seek or make an occupation for themselves. Do I need now, to tell any one who hears me, that it is out of such a condition of things that there is sure to arise, sooner or later, every imaginable evil that can afflict society or ruin the individual soul? Have we read history so little or so poorly that we do not know that, given the growth of luxury, wealth, and indolence, and straightway you have prepared a nest in which a whole brood of vices will soon and swiftly be hatched? When one home is clouded or shattered by the shame of some wretched intrigue, and another stung and wounded by the cruelty of some causeless calumny, and a third dishonored and disbanded perhaps by some foolish and criminal extravagance, have we ever paused to consider amid what idleness, what aimlessness, amid what vapid seeking for a fresh excitement in the dead dull level of an unemployed and uninterested life, these manifold forms of evil were conceived and initiated? Ah! if we could trace back some crime or shame or baseness to its incipient beginning, how often should we find it true that, into the life "empty, swept and garnished," there had entered, just because it was so empty, its hands so idle and unemployed, its heart so uninterested and indifferent, a whole legion of devils to drag it down to hell. We are wont, some of us, to pity the poor and have much to say of that sympathy which is the due of the tired day-laborer. And, God knows, the poor often enough need our pity, and our brother man who works for his daily bread with his hands, earns with his day's wages often, our heartiest sympathy. But I have sometimes thought that far more fitting objects for our pity than the poor, were the rich and the idle. It is a hard fate to have to fight for one's livelihood among the surging competitions of a great city, and to know that if you faint and fall, there is but scant compassion to pause and help you on your feet again; but to live a life empty of all occupation—to have the doors and windows of one's soul open to any evil influence that may care to enter, to be a prey to every allurement that may beckon to us, and thus to be in daily danger of having one's life taken possession of by any vagrant passion, any demon of evil that may discover its weakness and its emptiness, this, surely, is the saddest and most perilous lot of all. We envy his life who is freed from the burden of toil, and whose neck is no longer galled by the collar of a daily task. But whose sleep is the sweetest think you, whose waking hours are the purest and least clouded by guilty or unwholesome visions, his whose days are crowded so full of honest and healthy tasks that he has no room for dreaming, or his whose dragging hours are at once empty of effort and empty of aspiration? Pity if you will the poor toiler whose scanty wages just suffice to keep the wolf from the door, and to whom the approach of old age is a Nemesis which means impaired powers, and reduced earnings and it may be downright dismissal itself; but then remember how the hard discipline of such a life as that is educating him who lives it to look and long with an intensity which you and I from our different standpoints can not even dream of, for the coming of a day when at length the weary worker,

> "Dropping the irksome task from out the tired hands,
> And, drawing the curtains on this darkened world,
> Shall close the weary eyes, and, with a patient sigh
> Murmuring, 'Our Father'—fall on sleep till dawn!"

Yes, think of such an one, taught by every hardship of this present life, to look, and long, aye, and to live for, a freer and a nobler life, and then think of that other who, walking without set tasks, or heavy burdens, has lived an empty, aimless life, his soul the ever-accessible resort of every evil spirit that

could taint its purity or degrade its aspirations,—
think of such an one, I say, given over at last to
be the slave of every frivolous, selfish, self-indulgent
impulse and desire, growing old and gray-headed
with no faith in humanity and no trust in God, and
then tell me which of these two classes most deserves our pity or most urgently claims our prayerful
sympathy!

And if any of us here this morning belongs in
any sense to the latter of them, if, in other words,
there are any of us whose days have no other occupation than that which we ourselves make, let
us awaken at once to the perils and to the privilege of our position. Those perils I have indicated,
already, even as our own experience has, I am sure,
taught them to a great many of us. But over against
such perils, stand those privileges with which so
often God as it were balances and harmonizes the
inequalities of our life, and which make it possible for
us to make of that life so blessed and noble a thing.
Remember then, if your hands are empty and your
hours unemployed, how many gracious and beautiful
tasks God has set for your doing right here where
you stand. Sometimes, you know, in order to escape
as thoroughly as possible out of the atmosphere of
their wonted life, the dwellers in cities will seek in summer-time the plain fare and rough couch and rude conveniences of the camp-life of the hunter in the woods,

and never are so happy as when, after beating the streams, or climbing the hills all day, they come back hungry and tired at nightfall to eat with keenest relish the simplest fare, and then to lie down straightway to the blessed but unfamiliar boon of sweet and dreamless sleep. We are wont to explain the charm of such a life by saying that it is a transient return to that primitive barbarism toward which there is in every one, howsoever highly civilized, a lingering though latent tendency. But I think that often we should find a truer explanation of its charm in the more obvious fact of its hard work and wholesome simplicity. To be so healthily tired-out by a day of genuine activity that one craves no sensational amusement to beguile him and has neither interest nor appetite for any unwholesome excitement to make him forget the mere tedium of living, this surely, is an inexpressible boon. And such a boon, thank God, is after all within the reach of every one of us. There is good, wholesome, blessed and surely rewarding work to be done in all these streets and homes, these hospitals and asylums of ours, to keep us all busy and make us all thankful, for the privilege of rest and repose. There are problems enough to be solved to keep all of us who have any leisure at all well and wisely employed,—problems which never will be solved by mere alms-giving or institutionalism, or by any thing less than the living, loving co-operation of living hearts and hands. Into such channels of endeavor, if ours is in any sense a life of leisure, let us resolve in the Master's name to turn the stream of our activities. Into the lives that are to-day empty, swept, and garnished, let us ask Him, first of all, to come and abide Himself. And then, when He has illumined their darkness with the light of His own presence, and quickened their sluggishness with the fires of His own love, then let us turn to Him,—not to society nor our neighbor, nor any base power of evil that stands waiting to take us captive,—and cry straight up into His listening ear, "Lord, what wilt Thou have me to do?" Believe me, He will show us our work and give us strength and courage to begin it.

And if, on the other hand, our lot is one with scanty leisure and with many tasks, let us not bemoan or regret it. I speak to some this morning whose lives are all marked out for them by the hard exigencies of some narrow round of duty from which they may scarce step a single pace. There are clerks tied to their desks or shut in behind their counters who are among those who hear me this morning as I rejoice to know, and who as I can easily imagine have listened to this hasty sketch of an empty and unemployed life almost with a feeling of amused wonder. They do not think a little more leisure would involve any particular peril to them; and possibly it would not. Yet you may well rejoice, my brother, in any honest task that fills your day so full that the devil has only your evenings in which to get a chance at you, and you may wisely remember that in the honest doing of that task you have as worthy a field for loyal service of the Master as can anywhere be found. Honest work, well done for duty's sake, what is that but another name for what the apostle means when he says, "not with eye service, as men-pleasers, but in singleness of heart, fearing God."

And so of others who are not men but women. There are some such in this congregation who are teachers (that noble army of martyrs of whom, no more to-day, than in the beginning, is the world worthy), and who, by that, or by some other equally exacting obligation of place or task, are held hard down all day long, week in and week out, to work which they may not intermit and dare not neglect. Let even such I say thank God for the duty, aye, even the drudgery, that keeps them safe from perils that they do not dream of. Any thing, any thing is better than an aimless, unoccupied life!

And therefore, O Thou who when Thou wast in the world didst say to Thy disciples, "I must work the works of Him that sent me, while it is day. The night cometh when no man can work," fill our emptiness, our aimlessness with Thyself. And then, for all the tasks that Thou settest us to do, give us both strength and patience till the end!

SERMON XIX.

AMUSEMENTS.

ECCLESIASTES III. 1, 4.

"To every thing there is a time: . . . . a time to weep and a time to laugh;
a time to mourn and a time to dance."†

AND this, simply because the times and seasons of a life must needs answer to the changing phases and impulses of that life itself. If one set of experiences brings with it the mourning impulse, another will surely bring the laughing impulse;—nay, so close together, as the poet tells us, lie the fountains of tears and of mirth, that we may pass from the one to the other with scarce a moment's intermission.

Even so of every other phase of human feeling. It will have, it was meant to have, expression. The play impulse is, I verily believe, as sacred in the Divine intention as the work impulse. Indeed, a great thinker * has undertaken to show how what he calls the state of play is the ultimate state of redeemed and regenerated humanity, up to which it climbs through previous discipline in the working state; and though

---

* New York, March 3d, 1872.
† Dr. Bushnell.

in his argument he has not actually done so, yet I presume he would regard that prophetic picture of the new heavens and the new earth wherein Zechariah declares that "the streets of Jerusalem shall be full of boys and girls playing in the streets thereof" as only a poetic description of the heavenly employments of children of a larger growth. For, when we come to look a little deeper than the surface, what do we mean by play? Coming home at the end of the day, weary and worn and fretted, you open the door upon your little one rolling and tumbling upon the floor with a kitten. It is certainly not a very classical nor a very dignified scene, and yet, somehow, your heart straightway softens to it, and you sit down and watch the romp with a sense of sympathy and refreshment that you have not had through all the dull and plodding day. Why is it? Why, but because after all that is life without effort or care or burden, joy without labor or rivalry or tedium, bounding motion and bubbling glee without anxiety and without remorse! And what is such a life, disengaged from its animal characteristics and ennobled by a spiritual insight, but the true idea of heaven, where, if there be activity, there will be no effort, but where all that we do and are will be the free spontaneous outburst of the overflowing joy and gladness that are in us.

To attempt to extirpate the play side of life, then, is at once an absurdity and an impossibility. Because

the wise man has said that "the laughter of fools is as
the crackling of thorns under a pot," we may not hastily conclude that we are not to heat the cold gruel
of our daily drudgery or care with any mirth at all, for
if we did, we should be straightway confronted with
that other scripture which declares that "a merry
heart doeth good like a medicine." It has been said
that man is the only animal that laughs, and if so,
then laughter is a signature of his immortality, and
connects him directly with a being and a career alike
immeasurably above the present. If the child will
not smile, then our affectionate solicitude straightway
deepens into anxious foreboding, for we know that
the smile is the healthful expression of child-life, that
it should throw off its shouts of baby glee as freely as a
full fountain tosses its glittering spray athwart the sun-
light; and when a man passes into that stage where
his work engrosses and absorbs him so that he will
not stop for recreation, and has, as he gruffly tells
you, no time for amusement, then we sadly feel that
one side of him, and that not the lowest nor the meanest side, has grown prematurely numb and torpid.

But in truth, there is little need of reminding ourselves of all this in our generation, for, whatever may
have been the heresies of some who went before us, in
regard to this matter of the place and function, in a
healthy and also in a Christian life, of that ingredient
which we call amusement, such heresies have long ago

been thoroughly and even rudely exploded. We have all of us had our derisive jest over the blue-laws of our ancestors, and there is a sort of swaggering complacency in much of the speech and more of the action of our day, as they assert their equal independence and indifference concerning what are called the foolish and puritanical austerities of the olden time. Indeed, the danger at present is rather in the direction of what may be called the deification of amusement. "People must be entertained," we are told, with almost a tone of threatening in the declaration, as though it were meant, "woe be to him who, with any adverse theory, gets in the way of the popular tide which is setting in towards larger measures of amusement! Men may preach as they please, but people, and especially young people, will have amusement."

For one I say, by all means let them have it; but I have not so poor an opinion of most young persons, or most old persons either, as to believe that the one or the other of these classes is utterly reckless and indifferent to the questions, why and how they shall amuse themselves. For, after all, the same heart and brain that include the play faculty and the mirth-emotion include that other and supreme faculty which we call conscience, and if I could at this moment summon before you some young life that is this very afternoon seeking what it blindly calls amusement among scenes that I may not name here, and amid companionships whose forced and fitful gaiety is like the gleam of a flickering candle within a grinning skull, how unequivocally would such an one confess to you, how, if he could, he would gladly exchange all that he now calls pleasure for one day's experience of the innocency and peace of his youth. Yes, verily, these natures of ours do want amusement, but they want it in its rightful place and measure, and in due subordination to some healthful and Christian law.

Let us inquire then (*a*) what is that place which amusement ought to occupy in every healthful and well-ordered life? and also (*b*) what are the requirements of that law by which our amusement ought to be governed?

I. In speaking of amusement in its rightful place and measure, it is plainly enough implied that mere amusement ought not to be, and can not healthfully be the end of any life. We speak of child-life as the play-period of a human existence. And yet, have you never noticed that even the child can not play, unless he has climbed up into the sphere of play, through the toilsome vestibule of work? We see him careering over the ground in the wild joy of his young freedom, climbing the trees, scaling the hillsides, racing through the fields, or gambolling on the grass, and we say, "what glad surrender to pure impulse!" But do we remember how he has come to that free command of himself, his limbs and lungs and muscles; how he has tottered first of all, on his tiny feet, and fallen, and risen, only to fall again; how by slow gradations he has taught his muscles to obey his will, and his feet to do the bidding of his thought, and his hands to grasp and hold the things he reaches after? Not without effort, surely, has he come into that larger freedom of the first play state; and not without work, as his best qualification for the really sacred privilege of amusement, has God meant that any one of us should come to our playing moments!

And the best evidence of this, is to look at those who have made amusement not a means to an end, not a recreation (how happy and descriptive is the word, re–creation), of the fagged and wearied powers, but an aim to which all other things must needs give way! "Go and see the clown, Grimaldi, and laugh and get well," said Abernethy to a man who came to consult him concerning an attack of morbid and almost hopeless hypochondria. "I am the clown, Grimaldi," was the gloomy and staggering response, from one who had found the business of being perpetually and professionally funny, the dreariest and most melancholy career which a human being could well have undertaken. Even so of those who are perpetually seeking, not to amuse, but to be amused. Nay, their case is apt to be even worse and more discouraging. For they are making no effort for others, but simply selfishly waiting to be played upon, and so provoked to laugh without ever having earned the right to smile. And so, in point of fact, they rarely do either. One sees a great variety of life and character in this eager hurrying world of ours; but I put it to your own experience, are there to be found anywhere, more stolid, unimpressible, indifferent or peevish people, than those whose end and aim in life is mere amusement? Every thing drags with such persons, and because they can not be roused to such a thing out of their torpid impassiveness, a genuine hearty, ringing laugh has come to be with them a kind of indecorum to be greeted with a well-bred stare of cold and stony surprise. Happy would it be for such persons if they could be shaken out of their indolent selfishness long enough to learn that the true joy of play can never come till we have prefaced it with something of earnest and self-forgetting work. If one would know the real zest of being amused, let him put his hands or his brain or his heart, first of all to some manly or womanly task for himself or others, or for his Divine Master, and then the play-hour will come to him as music to a tired brain, and the jaded mind will turn itself out into the pleasure of the moment with the same exuberant delight in change and freedom as the schoolboy's, when he springs from his desk and bursts forth into the open air and sunshine. Plainly, the very first question that stands over against this whole subject of amusement is this—Are you and I entitled to any amusement at all? Have we any cares or burdens or duties from which we may now and then wisely and healthfully turn and ask that the bent bow shall be for a little unstrung, the tense strain of effort or of anxiety for a while be relaxed? or are we after all but "idlers in the mighty school of life," longing only to be beguiled out of the tedium of our indolence, and to have our pleasure-jaded and surfeited natures thrilled by a fresh sensation? If so, then verily we shall find ourselves disappointed in whatsoever amusement we may seek, as in truth we most surely deserve to be.

II. But again, having thus recognized what must needs be the one inflexible condition precedent to the seeking of any amusement, the question still remains, what are the principles that ought to regulate our amusements? To that question I would briefly answer, those principles are threefold. Our amusements ought to be genuine, innocent and moderate.

(*a*) Let me explain what I mean by a genuine amusement. If amusement has, as we have seen, a definite and recognizable place in every healthful and well-ordered life—if it is something to which we may turn, not merely as innocently but as wisely as one may turn to his daily private devotions, (and it is plain that to look at it in any other light, to make it something merely to be winked at, or reluctantly tolerated, is straightway to take the first step toward all manner of license,) then we must at least require of· it that it shall honestly serve its purpose—that it shall really and veritably recreate, re–create us. Now, viewed in this light, I do not, *e. g.*, call a ball a genuine amusement. I say nothing now of the function which an assemblage, gathered at an hour when people are ordinarily in their beds, in over-heated, over-crowded rooms, under conditions hopelessly unfavorable to hearty or kindly intellectual intercourse, aiming simply and supremely at physical and millinery display, may answer in the sphere of what is conventionally known as "society," for I confess frankly that the whole subject is to me a mystery, which, the more it is scrutinized only grows the more obscure and unintelligible; but I protest against the calling of such an entertainment, or of any other form of recreation with such characteristics, by the name of genuine amusement. Our amusements ought to leave us fresher and brighter than they found us, not jaded and irritable and lack-lustre eyed when the next day's duties roll back upon us. And therefore, I do not wonder that a great many young persons especially, who seek their amusements (heaven save the mark!) in such channels, are constrained to "key themselves up" to work, by the artificial means of unhealthy stimulants.

(*b*) But again; if amusement is not something outside but inside the sanctions of an earnest and Christian life, then our amusements ought also to be innocent. In such a discussion as this I can only touch
upon salient points, and so I go straightway from the
question of innocent amusements in the abstract to
that concrete presentation of the issue which is afforded
in the amusements that are about us. One of the most
conspicuous of these is the drama, and its lawfulness
as a recreation is much discussed at all times. "The
Bible does not forbid the theatre," it is said. Very
true. "The drama may be the vehicle of very lofty
and ennobling lessons." Very true again. "Every
body reads and the preacher quotes the immortal
plays of Shakespeare. Why should not we see those
plays enacted?" Again the plea is a plausible one,
and true as far as it goes. But we must remember
that those of us who state the case thus are stating
not a real but an ideal case. The concern of one who
is deciding the question between amusements that are
innocent and those that are not innocent, is with the
drama as he actually and ordinarily finds it; and this includes the drama whether classic or tragic or comic, or
seminude and spectacular; and if any complain that the
Church of God frowns upon innocent amusements, and
if it utters no downright condemnation, at least with-
holds its approval from innocent forms of amusement,
let them remember that it is because ordinarily those

who have once crossed a certain line in this matter, no matter what may be their professions of decorum or religion, are far too commonly wont to cast all restrictions utterly and absolutely behind them. For there is in fact almost absolutely no pretence of discrimination in these things, and persons of pure lives and unspotted name are seen, in our day, gazing upon spectacles or hearkening to dialogues, which, whether spoken or sung, ought to bring a blush of shame to any decent cheek. If we could see some parent rising in her seat in a place of public amusement and calling those about her to follow her out of it, when both modesty and decorum had been outraged by the mimic scene upon the stage, we should have a specimen of genuine heroism which would go farther than any thing else to give us healthful and innocent dramatic representations. But alas, who of us ever hears of such noble boldness as this? and since those who ought soonest to do so, exercise no wise discrimination and put forth no healthful influence in this matter, is it any wonder that the Church can only look silently and often sadly on? Most assuredly, I do not presume to be conscience for any other human being; and the single issue in the matter of the innocence of your amusements is undoubtedly, are they innocent, not for me, but for you? But we may not dare to push the question wholly and absolutely aside. If we can not be amused without vulgarizing our speech, and dissipating our minds and debauching our morals, then, no matter what we are called upon to give up, we had better go on plodding in the dull round until we drop weary and lifeless in our tracks.

(c) But, let us also remember, amusement may be thoroughly innocent in its nature, and yet very easily be excessive or immoderate in its measure. We Americans, if we work at all, are apt to work very hard, and it is undoubtedly true that the great mass of our countrymen have too infrequent holidays and play too little. But just because of this, or because of our somewhat intense and eager national temperament our amusements are not uncommonly, though innocent enough in themselves, pursued with an excessive devotion which at once alters their character and largely impairs their benefits. The past few years have witnessed an illustration of this in an enthusiasm for out-door sports which, promising exceedingly well at the outset, soon degenerated into an intense and often unseemly rivalry, in which what was originally intended as a pastime became with many persons a profession, and which has been associated far too widely with our national passion of gambling—a passion which has so corrupted many forms of intrinsically innocent amusement as virtually to exclude from them almost every scrupulous and self-respecting person. To return to the wisdom of that testament with which we began, if there is a time for innocent and wholesome amusement, it must be content to consume only its own time and to stay within its own limits.

And now, a word in conclusion. What is that which is wanted first and most to guide us in the application of these principles? Is it a definite code of church discipline? Is it a perpetual reference to what people about us will say? Surely we ought to have found out by this time that neither of these restraints has ever proved itself of any practical worth. In other days civil governments have enacted sumptuary laws to restrain the popular extravagance, but the people whom they were meant to restrict were always able to find ways, many and easy, by which to evade such laws. Or, shall we go just so far as current sentiment tacitly admits that a Christian man or woman may go in their amusements and stop when the world objects? Verily this is like that person who, when reproached for his attendance upon some scene of gaiety soon after the death of his wife, excused himself on the ground that he had asked his wife's mother if she had any objections, and she had said she had not! Such love or such reverence for another's memory we should probably say was worth but very little, and surely to act from such motives in dealing with our Maker and our Master must be worth a

great deal less. And therefore what is wanted to
guide us in the question of our amusements is first
of all and most of all a heart deep in the love of
Christ—a character sanctified by the life and sunshine of the Holy Spirit. We may then commit
errors of judgment, but we shall not be forgetful
of our loyalty nor our love. And then, with whatsoever zest we turn from work to play (and, remember, the apostle bids us "whatsoever ye do, do
it heartily,") we shall then, I say, find in all the
joy and play and freedom of our resting moments
here, the antitype and foretaste of the perfect joy
and bliss and freedom of the better life beyond.

SERMON XX.

COST AND BEAUTY IN CHRISTIAN WORSHIP.

2 CHRONICLES III. 6; IV. 21.

" And he garnished the house with precious stones, for beauty; and the gold was the gold of Parvaim."

" And the flowers, and the lamps, and the tongs made he of gold, and that perfect gold." *

THE author of the history of the Jewish Church uses these words concerning the Temple of Solomon: "As in the Grecian tragedies we see always in the background the gate of Mycenæ, so in the story of the people of Israel we have always in view the Temple of Solomon. There is hardly any Jewish reign that is not in some way connected with its construction or its changes. In front of the great Church of the Escurial in Spain,—in the eyes of Spaniards itself a likeness of the temple—overlooking the court called from them the Court of the Kings, are six colossal statues of the Kings of Judah who bore the chief part in the Temple of Jerusalem—David the proposer; Solomon the founder; Jehoshaphat, Hezekiah, Josiah, Manasseh, the successive purifiers and restorers. The idea there so impressively graven in stone runs

---

* New York, October 13th, 1878.

through all the subsequent history"* of the chosen
people.

It is of this Temple, so integral a part of the life of
the Hebrew commonwealth that the words I have
quoted from the book of the Chronicles are spoken,
and I have chosen them because they are an intimation of that one truth which was a clew to the whole
construction.

Why was the Temple of Solomon built, and what
was the motive especially of its enormous costliness
and its unrivalled beauty? It was built, as we know,
under divine direction and, in every least detail, in
accordance with divine command. If it had been
otherwise, if we had read in this book of the Chronicles that it was built simply in accordance with the
inspiration of Solomon's love of magnificence or ambition for display,—if it had simply been said in connection with all this lavish outlay of human skill and
gold and precious stones, "Thus did Solomon, thus
and so," we should have been constrained to regard it
much as we are accustomed to think of the Pyramids
or of any more recent monument of human art and
grandeur. But what Solomon did, is preceded, with
respect to every least detail, by the clear intimation
of what Solomon was commanded to do. Solomon
did not "garnish the house with precious stones, and

---

* Stanley's "Lectures on the Jewish Church," 2d series.

with gold of the gold of Parvaim," because he was ambitious as a king and a conqueror to outshine his neighbors or to immortalize himself, but because he was bidden to do so. When we turn to the first of those chapters in the Chronicles from which I have quoted, we read, "These are the things wherein Solomon was instructed for the building of the house of God," and then follow those precise details to which the text refers.

In other words, the temple was not an exhibition of wealth or cleverness, or superiority on the part of man its builder, it was man's education in cost and sacrifice and unsparing labor, on the part of God its designer. There is just one principle that runs through all the teaching of the two Testaments concerning what men do for their Maker, and that is that God does not want, and can not otherwise than lightly esteem that which costs us nothing, and that the value of any service or sacrifice which we render for His sake, is, that, whatever may be its intrinsic meanness or meagreness, it is, as from us, our very best, not given lightly or cheaply or unthinkingly, but with care and cost and crucifixion of our self-indulgence; and then again, that it is such gifts, whether they are the adornment of the temple, or the box of alabaster, filled with ointment of spikenard very precious and spilled wastefully as Christ's own disciples account it upon their Master's feet; or, again the myrrh and spices with which a broken-hearted devotion embalmed that same Master's dead body—that these are gifts that God equally and always delights in.

Equally and always, I say, and this is the point for us who are here this morning. It is commonly argued that whatever may have been the appropriateness of that earlier devotion which built and beautified the temple, it is superannuated, inappropriate, and even (as some tell us) unwarranted now. Those costly and almost barbaric splendors, it is said, were appropriate to a race in its infancy, and to a religion in the germ. But the temple and the ritual of Judaism have flowered into the sanctuary and the service of the Church of Christ. Not to Mount Gerizim nor Jerusalem do men need to journey to worship the Father, says the Founder of that Church Himself. "God is a Spirit, and they that worship Him must worship Him in spirit and in truth." If one would show his devotion to Him, says this same divine Teacher, "sell all that thou hast and give to the poor." It is not to adorn temples and garnish holy places that Christianity is called nowadays, but to rear hospitals, and shelter orphans and feed the hungry. It is a diviner thing to send bread to some starving household or to minister, in some plague-smitten Memphis or New Orleans, to some fevered sufferer, than to build all the altars and adorn all the sanctuaries that ever were reared!

No! it is not—not one whit diviner—noble and Christ-like as such service surely is. Let us come to a distinct understanding here as to an issue concerning which, in the popular mind, there is much confusion and much more misapprehension.

If it is asked, is there not an order and sequence in which things equally excellent may wisely and rightly be done, the answer is plain enough. If any body is starving or houseless or orphaned, the first thing to do is to feed and shelter and succor them. And so long as such work is undone, we may wisely postpone other work, equally meritorious and honorable. But it should be clearly understood that if in some ages, a disproportionate amount of time and money and attention have been given to the æsthetics of religion, in others the same disproportion has characterized that which has been given to what may justly be called the sentimentalism of religion. It is possible—nay, why do I state the question hypothetically—it is dismally certain that an enormous amount of indiscriminate alms-giving both in our own and other generations has bred only shiftlessness, indolence, unthrift, and even downright vice. It was indiscriminate alms-giving that bred the whole pestilent race of mendicant frairs in the thirteenth century, and if any one wants to know what was the influence of these orders on the social and domestic life of their times, he need only read the ballads of

Chaucer and the pages of Mr. Lecky to learn. I do not hesitate to say that it would have been infinitely better if all the cost and expenditure which propagated and pampered those liveried vagabonds had been spent in most useless ornamentation (as we are accustomed to reckon such things) upon the most obscure sanctuaries in Christendom, and as little do I hesitate to say that there has been and still is an enormous amount of ill-judged and misdirected almsgiving in our day, which has done more harm and wrought more degradation in human nature than the tawdriest ornamentation upon the most tinsel-clap and bedizened altar anywhere to be found. God forbid that we should hastily close our hand or our hearts against any needier brother! But God most of all forbid that we thrust him down into a condition of chronic pauperism by the wanton and selfish facility with which we buy our privilege of being comfortably let alone by him with an alms or a dole. Better a thousand times, I say, that our gifts should enrich a cathedral already thrice adorned, and clothe its walls already hung with groaning profusion of enrichment, for then at least, some one coming after us may be prompted to see and own that, whatever fault of taste or congruity may offend him, there has not been building and beautifying without cost and sacrifice.

And this brings me to the thought to which especially, I wish to give expression, to-day. Since many of us last assembled in this place it has been garnished with precious stones, and enriched by the costly sculptures which have I trust gladdened and delighted all our eyes. The holy table, on which last Sunday my brother and associate placed for the first time the symbols of the Master's love, and around which some of us here present drew near to kneel, is worthier of the sacred uses to which, by that act, it was set apart, than any thing which we have heretofore possessed. Of its meetness and beauty for its sacred uses I hope we are not in doubt, but of the necessity for any such erection, and still more concerning all the very considerable cost and expenditure which have accompanied it, there may be some of us, I can not but think, who may easily be perplexed. And while therefore it is not unnatural that on returning here after a somewhat lengthened absence, I should congratulate myself and you upon the successful completion of a work so beautiful in itself and so singularly harmonious with its surroundings, it is not unfitting that I should say something of the motives that have inspired and directed it.

There have been expended here, during the past summer, in the adornment and enriching of this sanctuary, several thousands of dollars, which have neither enlarged our accommodations nor multiplied our services, nor appreciably increased any body's fa-

would somehow be transfigured into a symbol of unselfish thoughtfulness for others. But it is because, too often, our dress, our houses, our entertainments, our equipages, are only so many means by which we strive to outshine and eclipse our neighbor, that such expenditure becomes so largely not only the wasteful, but the truly contemptible thing that it is. And yet it is no wonder that so long as we allow such motives to influence us in things secular, we should infer or impute them concerning things that are sacred.

And therefore it is that any such motive ought here, and especially in connection with the expenditure which has lately been made in this holy house, to be utterly and indignantly repudiated. We aim here at no rivalry, nor at any competitive triumph.

II. And as little, let me also say, are we influenced by another and somewhat kindred motive of which one hears much in our day. When changes are made in our social customs, in our habits of expenditure, and even in our modes of worship, we are often told that they are necessitated because we must "keep up with the times," and those who are wedded by very sacred associations to things ancient, are often wounded in their tenderest feelings by being told that they must give up the old in order not to be behind the age, in order to be in accord with the

spirit of the nineteenth century. Well, the spirit of
the nineteenth century, whatever else may be said
of it, is not an infallible spirit, and in many respects
it would be better if some of us were behind the age,
rather than so eagerly and unthinkingly in accord with
it. But however this may be, the "spirit of the age"
can never be the guide for the principles of worship
or the law of sacrifice. These must be determined by
an authority infinitely higher and more stable.

III. Once more, it will probably be said, however,
that the enriching and beautifying of Christian sanctuaries finds its motive in making those sanctuaries
more helpful because of such cost and beauty, to the
instinct of worship and devotion. And undoubtedly
such a motive is a perfectly valid and intelligible one.
A building does influence the mind of him who stands
or kneels in it, and no one who has entered those
hoary monuments of the faith and patience of the
Middle Ages which we know as the cathedrals of
the old world, can have been wholly insensible to
that influence.

But while it is true that some stately minster like
Durham or Rouen, or some exquisite crystallization
in fretted marbles like Bayeux in Normandy, or Salis-
bury in England, hushes with a sense of instinctive
awe and wonder and reverence, the footsteps and
the heart-beat of him who enters it; it is not until we

come closer to those wonderful buildings that we find the loftiest motive that inspired those who reared them, and equally, that loftiest motive that ought, in any similar work, to inspire us to-day. For it is not until we come closest to them—not until we have climbed their heights and gone down into their depths, and pushed our way into uncounted hidden and out of the way corners, and passages, and galleries—that we see how those wonderful men of an earlier generation toiled singly and supremely to give to God their best, and to spend their art and toil where, often if not ordinarily, it could be seen and owned and adequately appreciated, by no other eye than His.

And this I maintain is alone the one sufficient motive for cost, and beauty, and even lavish outlay, in the building and adornment of the house of God to-day. It is a motive to which we, in America, with our merely utilitarian spirit have hardly even begun to awaken. And as a consequence of it, we have not to-day, in all this broad land of ours, one single ecclesiastical building, that is really worthy of the enormous wealth of the country, or of the widespread luxury of its inhabitants. We may well rejoice therefore and be thankful when any Christian disciple strives anywhere to do any thing that tells out to God and men, whether in wood, or stone, or gold, or precious stones, that such an one would fain

consecrate to Him the best and costliest that human
hands can bring. When any poor penuriousness cries
out upon such an outlay, "To what purpose is this
waste?" the pitiful objection is silenced by that answer of the Master's to her who broke above His
feet the alabaster box of ointment, very precious,
"Verily I say unto you, wheresoever throughout the
whole world this gospel shall be preached, this thing
that this woman hath done shall be told for a me-
morial of her." And why was it to be told? for the
spreading of her fame? No, but for the inculcation
of her example.

For this, after all, is the very essence of the cross
of Christ,—this is the gospel itself,—a love that does
not count the cost, a sacrifice that does not haggle
about the outlay, a devotion so utter and so absolute that were the whole realm of nature ours with
which to repay it, our best and choicest would still
be too poor to give.

What is the power of Calvary over men? That it
was an eternally necessary sacrifice — that in no
other way could God have saved the race, than in
the way which actually He chose? Once there was
a theology which uttered a dogma so bold and so
essentially presumptuous as this; but thank God, it
has long ago found its way to the crowded limbo of
outworn theological vagaries. No, the power of the
cross over men lies in this, that it is the gift to men,

by God, of His very best—"His well-beloved Son." And, when we turn from Calvary to those heroic lives that, as they gleam along the track of the Christian centuries seem to have drunk most deeply of the spirit of Calvary, what is it that most distinguishes these but that they gave to God their best,— the flower of their youth, the fresh fire of their genius, the full and utter devotion of their hearts? Turn where you will, from St. Paul the scholar, the enthusiast, and the peerless dialectitian, to John Coleridge Patterson the Oxford prizeman, the young Englishman of gentle lineage and brilliant prospects who flung away his life, as the world accounts of such sacrifices, among the brutal savages of Melanesia, this is the single characteristic that equally and everywhere adorns them.   And so, we may be sure that when the King who sits upon His throne above declares in those most pregnant words of prophecy, of those who have loved and served Him here, "and they shall be mine in that day when I make up my jewels," He means supremely those who have adorned that service with utmost sacrifice and with most unsparing cost.

Let us thank God, therefore, whenever He puts it into the hearts of any of His servants to do that which beautifies His holy house with unsparing cost and thoroughness.   The infirmity of too much of our building to-day is twofold: first, it is merely utilitarian, asking always, "What is the practical gain of it?" and so smothering that loftier instinct of beauty and richness which is, in its turn, so closely allied to the ardent and uncalculating spirit of a grateful worship; and, second, it is cheap and disingenuous, seeking imposing effects without adequate cost, and most of all deficient in solidity of material and thoroughness, and therefore costliness, of detail. It is a miserable spirit even at its best estate, and I rejoice that we have at length, in this sanctuary, something which, as an accessory of our Christian worship, implies cost, and witnesses in every least detail to an absolute thoroughness.

May it be the type and symbol of that which shall adorn our lives who come to worship here! Cost and thoroughness;—verily these are the traits for which the Christianity of our day is chiefly waiting. We have wordy professions, and effusive sentiment; would that we might have more of the spirit of thoroughness and the spirit of sacrifice. Our calling it is, the apostle reminds us, to be "built up as lively stones" into that spiritual house, reared upon the foundation of the apostles and prophets, of which Jesus Christ Himself is the chief corner-stone. Do we remember under what discipline of sorrow and persecution and self-surrender those first disciples were wrought and shaped, until they became as the polished corners of the temple? Still the stately and laborious process goes on. One after another, as their work of preparation is ended, God calls His servants home to take their place as living stones in His eternal temple. There is more than one place vacant here to-day, that was filled by its devout and reverent occupant when last I spoke to you from this place. The heads of households long honored and beloved among us, a citizen for half a century esteemed and respected at the bar, and another distinguished by his taste and enterprise in commerce and in letters, a mother who had seen well-nigh her whole household go up to their rest in Paradise before her, and another just on the threshold of life, who laid down that life in giving it to another,—these are among those whom we miss to-day, and whose absence clouds our joy as we kneel in this holy place.

But, blessed be God, theirs at last is the temple not made with hands, eternal in the heavens. And so, while we gather, glad that any one of us is permitted to beautify His holy house, and give Him of her best, be it ours to ask that He will teach us first of all to give ourselves to Him, and so, full of the life that fellowship with Him imparts, to count our choicest and our best as spent most worthily when they are spent for Him!

SERMON XXI.

FAITH AND CULTURE.

ECCLESIASTES I. 8; PSALM XXXIX. 7.

"All things are full of labor; man can not utter it: the eye is not satisfied with seeing, nor the ear filled with hearing."
"And now, Lord, what is my hope? Truly my hope is even in thee."
(Prayer Book version.) †

THE first of these two verses is the language of a man who had seen much of life, and who was equally eminent for his native penetration and his extraordinary learning. "The reign of Solomon, the author of this book of Ecclesiastes, has sometimes been called the Augustan age of the Jewish nation. But Solomon was to Israel not only its Augustus, but its Aristotle, and more than one oriental scholar has owned at least the high probability of that Rabbinical tradition which affirms that when Alexander the Great took Jerusalem, he captured the works of Solomon and sent them to Aristotle, who thence derived all that was good in his philosophy." *

The words of such a man would have a pre-eminent interest, even if they were ever so remote from our

---

* New York, Nov. 16th, 1879.
† Stanley, "Hist. of Jewish Church," vol. ii., p. 252.

own experience. But when you take the book of Ecclesiastes and read it as a whole, the strongest impression which it makes is that of its accuracy as a picture of the life of to-day. "All things are full of labor" runs the text, or to translate the thought that seeks expression in the words, "all things fatigue, and are full of burden and trouble."* It is the utterance of a tired mind, on which the restless movements of history, the ever-crowding sequence of events, the innumerable questions of philosophy, of science, of duty, and of pleasure, are all conspiring to press with endless and wearying iteration, and with indescribable rapidity and exhaustiveness. Is such an experience unfamiliar to most of us? Is the mind never staggered? does the brain never tire? are the overstrained sympathies never wrung out and unstrung? Are our capacities of enjoyment never sated and wearied by the manifold demands of the life of to-day? And is it not equally true that, crowd that life as full as we may with outward sensations, give the eye to see and the ear to hear every thing that ingenuity can discover or art depict, there is still a hunger for "that light that never was on land or sea," and still a hearkening for the sound that "ear hath not heard, neither hath it entered into the heart of man to conceive?"

And all this in spite of the fact that whatever life

* Ewald, Hengstenberg, Hahn, 12.

may have been in Solomon's day, it is an infinitely fuller and more various thing in ours. It is doubtless true that, in the light of a very imperfect knowledge of the older civilizations of the world we have been wont to impute to them an absence and an ignorance of many things which they both abundantly knew and possessed. Neither art nor science nor letters, we may wisely remember, were in their babyhood when Solomon built and beautified his capital, developed his commerce, and wrote his poetry and his prose. A closer study of those ancient civilizations which lie behind us and of their disentombed monuments and literature, equally rebuke the learning of our own generation and its pretensions. Sculpture, painting, poetry, architecture, the science of government and the principles of philosophy ascended to levels in the empires of Solomon and the Cæsars, in the senates and academies of ancient Greece and Rome to which they have not ascended since then. Solomon, Plato, Aristotle, Phidias, Julius Cæsar, Justinian,—these are names whose rank is as lofty and as unapproachable to-day as it was hundreds or thousands of years ago.

And yet, in the full consciousness of all this, we must still own that the life of man is a fuller, a more intense, a more many-sided thing to-day than ever before. How many interests it touches; amid what wide-reaching complications it lives and moves; under what enormous pressure it rushes on. The age which

we call our own has not been eminent for its thinking or conquering, but chiefly, if not exclusively, for
its inventing and contriving. It has annihilated the
distances that have separated nations and continents,
and made mechanical inventions the servants and
toilers for the many. Into the homes and habits of
our ancestors it has introduced a force which threatens utterly to transform our customs as well as our
houses. Is it this increasing disuse of the old ways
which makes us cling with such a fantastic eagerness
to the antiquated furniture and quaint utensils which
once sufficed those ancestors? Or is it the dawning
uncertainty as to whether, in letting go the old for
the new, we have really gained and have not, rather,
lost?

In a word, for that is the question to which our
text directly leads us, Is the world really happier
because of what civilization has done for it, or no?
We remember how our forefathers lived, and wonder, it may be, that they did not die of inanition.
Think of life without the morning newspaper and
the evening drama. Think of it without that electric contact between the nations of the whole round
world, which makes the evening indigestion of the
Porte or the Czar the morning topic of the American breakfast table. Think of life without our literature, so fertile, so diverting, so inquisitive, so affluent;
without our art, so ingenious, so realistic, so marvel-

lously adaptive; without our conveniences of travel and communication, and diversion, and cheap and almost universal luxury. Think of life without these things? The mind refuses thus to think of it! It looks back into those ruder ages in which the Saxon people, crossed and conquered by Norman and Dane, were laying the foundations of that mighty state from which our own is sprung, and as it sees how bald and bare life was of what, to so many of us, chiefly makes life now—as it sees how starved and empty the taste and imagination must needs have been—as it sees how ignorance and the inferiority of women and the servitude of whole classes and even races, prevailed, it protests with equal honesty and earnestness, that the world must needs be happier to-day than it ever was before.

I do not care too eagerly to dispute the proposition. It is a poor service which he renders to Christianity who insists that civilization has done nothing for the race and that there has been no progress in civilization apart from the progress of the Cross. Those two propositions are not, it may be, equally disputable; but that, in a sense, they may both be challenged, I think there can be no doubt. Civilization has done substantial service to humanity even apart from the religion of Christ, and, as history has plainly shown us, civilization is not necessarily Christian or even theistic. For what is a genuine civiliza-

tion, but a state of society which contributes to the
good order, intelligence, honesty, virtue and physical well-being of the people, and may there not be
a state of society in which all these things are the
fruit, not of religious teaching or of Christian faith,
but simply of an enlightened selfishness which has
found out that the individual is happier and better off
when the community is honest and healthy and mutually respectful and respecting? In admitting this
we need not leave out of sight the enormous influence which the religion of the New Testament as a
matter of fact has had in transforming and ennobling our civilization of to-day, any more than we
need refuse to recognize what the religion of Moses
did for the empire of Solomon. But conceding all
this, the question is, Would civilization disappear if
Christianity were to perish? Would culture cease to
be, if Christ ceased to be believed? Would society,
as you and I know it, lapse into barbarism, and the
life and manners of New York become the manners
of Zululand, without the knowledge of the faith of
the Crucified? I am by no means prepared to assert it.

But the question is, also, Would human happiness
remain? or rather, as I put it a moment ago, Is it
to civilization that the world owes its happiness, and
are we of to-day, with our higher and finer civilization,
happier than our forefathers? They were without a
multitude of advantages that we have, and the range

and the pace of their life, were almost infinitely narrower and slower. But in widening the range and in quickening the pace, have we deepened the current and enriched the quality of our lives? "Thou hast multiplied the nation," says the prophet, "and not increased the joy." There may be fulness, amplitude, multiplication, whether of numbers, wealth, luxury or culture, without a substantial increase of human happiness; and the question for us is, How far have all these things that conspire to make life more diversified and more entertaining, to occupy men less with their own thoughts and more with what is going on about them, to stimulate the imagination and challenge the inquisitiveness—how far have all these things contributed to make living, a more joyous, serene, contented and blessed thing? Candidly, must it not be owned that the old cry of the preacher-king, finds its echo in our hearts to-day? "All things are full of labor; man can not utter it." There is a bewildering multitude of interests and studies and problems that challenges our attention, there is a drain and pressure upon our sympathies, our power of attention, our capacity to distinguish and estimate, which sometimes, at any rate, fairly leaves one speechless, and underneath it all, shall we not own it, O my brothers, there is a straining of the eye, to see what no culture can disclose to it, and a hearkening of the ear for a tone which no human voice has ever spoken!

Why shall we not own it? I ask, for after all it is only owning that faith has its office and function in our lives as well as culture. There are times when the market is up, and times are good, and when all seems bright and fair. We know very well what we want at such times, and if we are quite candid we must own that there is not much that we want that we can not touch and taste and handle. But there are other times—times of reverses, of the pinch of adverse fortune, of the coldness of friends, of the death of the one being whom we loved—when it does not satisfy us that we can command a house with all the modern conveniences, and can cable to London in five minutes. Nay, there are moments in our prosperity, as well as in our adversity, when all that we have or can enjoy or can achieve, seems poor and pitiful beside the dream of what, ennobled by a mightier spell, we might become. Many a man has won the prize he strove for, only to find how poor and empty it was; and many another who has won no prize, striving for it eagerly all his life long, has been dimly conscious of that inmost deterioration as well as weariness, which has been the fruit of a life lived merely in the inspiration of an external civilization. Let it be admitted for the moment, if you choose, that there is in civilization a sufficient conservative force to preserve society from gross departures from the law of truth and right. Let it be admitted that culture and invention contribute enormously to the charm of living and to the comfort of it. Can it be said that culture or art or science take any cognizance, save as they had been made the handmaids of the Church, of the spiritual wants of man? You are tired, my brother, with the strife and rush and feverish hurry of your life. You are not calmed and steadied and uplifted by all this bustle of contrivance, of amusement, of acquisition that is going on about you. There is a sinking at your heart under the sunniest sky that may smile upon you, as you think of what may so easily happen to you. No lot, you know, is secure. No prosperity is indestructible. No life, no matter how incomparably dear and precious to you that life may be, is certain. These are facts which no civilization can build out of your horizon, nor any culture educate you to forget. And yet there is a Book which tells you of a life in which he who lives it, is "not afraid of any evil tidings, for his heart standeth fast and believeth in the Lord." There is a faith which has learned how to ask and to answer the deepest of all questions in the words, "And now, Lord, what is my hope? Truly my hope is even in Thee." There is a life—you know at least one or two who here and there are living it—in which the world is neither a charnel-house, nor its pleasures, dust and ashes; in which those who live it are not sad-faced nor morose nor cynical, but in which, also, there broods above its daily cares and hopes, that "peace that passeth understanding," and through which there thrill the melodies of a joy which, what men call the world, can never give and can never take away.

It is for this widening of the horizon of its life, that human society wants that message of faith which civilization does not and can not bring it. Stop a moment and think back through the week that ended with yesterday. What were the things that chiefly occupied our thoughts and hands, our eyes and ears? I am not saying that they were necessarily wrong things or unworthy things. But of this there can be very little doubt—they were mainly secular things. It is a common charge against excessive zeal in religion that it makes a man narrow and one-sided. But, did it ever occur to us that civilization may make a man equally narrow and one-sided? On any other than the atheistic theory of life, man is a spiritual being, meant to live mainly and supremely in a spiritual world. He is going to school here, and the things that he touches and sees and acquires here— his banks and railroads and factories, aye, and his books, his art, his æsthetic adornments and surroundings—all these are simply toys with which he is building block-houses in the nursery, until he is ripe enough and mature enough for the life and employments of the future.

And if this be so, what does he need? Nay, let us

make the question personal and concrete, What do we need so much as that message and those occasions which shall recall us from the outward and the transient, and lift us to the level of that broader culture which recognizes our relations, not merely to one world but to two? What do we need so much as a wisdom which shall teach us to see and to sing:

"The winds that o'er my ocean run,
   Reach through all worlds beyond the sun;
Through life and death, thro' faith, through time,
   Grand breaths of God, they sweep sublime.

"Eternal trades, they can not veer,
   And blowing teach us how to steer,
And well for him whose joy, whose care
   Is but to keep before them fair.

"O thou, God's mariner, heart of mine!
   Spread canvas to the airs divine;
Spread sail and let thy fortune be
   Forgotten in thy destiny.

. . . .

"A thread of law runs through thy prayer,
   Stronger than iron cables are;
And love and longing toward her goal,
   Are pilots sweet to guide the soul.

"So life must live, and soul must sail,
   And unseen over seen prevail;
And all God's argosies come to shore,
   Let ocean smile or rage or roar.

"And so mid storm or calm, my bark
 With snowy wake, still nears her mark;
 Cheerily the trades of being flow,
 And sweeping down the wind I go." *

It is to recall you to this higher range of thought
and aspiration that this holy house exists. What do
we come to church for if we do not need to be reminded, by what we see and hear and do here, of a
world and life outside the boundaries of the widest
civilization and unrevealed by the investigations of
the most painstaking culture? We have hopes that
are not met by any visible attainment. We have
fears that are not silenced by any earthly voice. And
there are some times when we have another and a
a more bitter consciousness—the consciousness of personal sin. We want to be forgiven. We want to be
renewed. We want to be emancipated. In one word,
we want that element in our lives which never enters
it until the cross has entered it, and has at once
conquered us by its love and transformed us by its
infinite and divine compassion.

We want all this, I say. Has it ever occurred to us
to think of those other lives who want it no less, and
who yet may so easily be left without it? To most
of those to whom I speak this morning this holy place,
these Christian ministrations, the leisure and the op-

---

* D. A. Wasson.

portunities (if only we care for them), for their constant enjoyment are things within easy command. We can own or hire our pew in church, we can command our time, at least on Sunday, and we can kneel and worship here, in at least reasonable security and comfort and repose.

But has it ever occurred to us to realize how difficult of attainment are what I may call the opportunities of cultivating the religious life among the poor? When one prays or meditates or reads his Bible, he wants the help of privacy in which to do it. But what privacy have the poor? What encouragement to a habit of prayer is there in a life in which ten or twelve people are often huddled together in two rooms? And when Sunday comes, what is to become of the poor man or woman who can neither own nor hire a pew, and whose bearing and attire too often make them strange and ill at ease in too many of our congregations? In building and maintaining, as this church has done, a free and open church for these classes, I do not say that we have done the best conceivable thing, but we have done the best thing that could be done under the circumstances. I am glad that it is my duty, to-day, to remind you of the existence of that free and open house of God, and to ask your help in maintaining its services. I should be thoroughly unhappy if the time ever came that our help would not be needed in maintaining those services. It is a most blessed and healthy bond between us and our less-favored brethren, which we need, believe me, even more than they do. Think what a free and open church offers for any soul that wants to recollect itself and to lift its thoughts to God! In our case, Grace Chapel is not merely open on Sundays, but all through the week. To-day it will gather within its walls congregations who will worship God in our tongue not only, but also in German, in Italian and Danish, for each of which nationalities there are separate services conducted in their own language. And on any and every day in the week, besides, from morning till evening its doors stand open, and any tired soul that will, may turn aside and rest there and commune with its own heart and with its Maker and be still.

Surely such an instrumentality claims our sympathy and deserves our help. Standing at the door of an Italian church, a young American traveller saw an aged woman vainly endeavoring to lift the heavy leathern curtain that stopped her entrance. It was a very natural and chivalrous instinct that prompted the youth to step forward and raise the portiere till the aged worshipper had passed within. But as she did so, she turned to him with the eager impulsiveness of her race and kissing the hand that held the uplifted curtain, exclaimed, "May God reward you, signor, and may an angel open for you the door of the upper Paradise!" To her God's house was the lower

Paradise. Who shall say to how many faint and hungry and sorrow-stricken ones it is no less, here and among us? Reach out, then, your hand, and help to open and to keep open a door where any and every weary heart may come and rest, and where, amid the roar and the hurry of the world's great life, the souls whose earthly hopes have failed of realization, may learn to say, with farther-reaching wisdom than the world can teach or tell, "And now, Lord, what is my hope? Truly my hope is even in Thee."

SERMON XXII.

THE ULTIMATE TEMPLE.

I KINGS VI. 7.

"And the house when it was in building was built of stone made ready before it was brought thither: so that there was neither hammer nor axe, nor any tool of iron, heard in the house while it was in building." *

WE look back at those ruder ages, as we call them, of which the Bible tells us, with considerable complacency, if not sometimes with contempt. We have learned so much that they never knew. Yes. And they did so much that we would never dare even to attempt. They built an empire out of barbarism. And we have simply adorned a civilization which we inherited from our forefathers. They developed a religion out of the most utter Paganism, and we have not added a single fundamental truth to the teaching of Moses. All that we have in our laws and beliefs and anticipations, existed in the seed, if not in the flower, in those principles which Moses brought down with him from the summit of Sinai.

In like manner, we think that we could teach those rude Hebrews of the elder dispensation a great many lessons as to the science of life. If they had an archi-

---

* New York, Feb. 29, 1880 (Mid-Lent).

tecture, it must, we imagine, have been vastly inferior to ours of to-day. But the imagination is sometimes over-active, and in this case, we shall be wise not to allow it to mislead us. The undertaking described in the text is what may be called a feat in architecture; and, in the history of architecture, it is simply and absolutely without a parallel. The Temple of Solomon was perhaps the most splendid and stately building that the world has known. Every costliest material—wood, stone, or precious metal—that architecture can employ was employed in its construction. That construction required the most colossal foundations, the most intricate contrivance, the utmost elaboration of details. And all this was achieved, and the whole building was lifted into its place, with no sound of any tool nor blow of a single hammer.

It may be said that such an achievement is possible to architecture to-day. But it never has been accomplished. Great buildings are constantly reared in which the stone is quarried and dressed in Maine the timbers felled and hewn in Georgia, and the iron work forged and wrought in Pennsylvania or New Jersey. But these structures are not fitted together, nor reared upon their foundations without noise and blows and manifold sounds of coercion. Now then, noise is one of the curses of life. In crowded centres of population it is probably the cause of as much constant torture as is suffered in time of war on a great

battle-field. We get scarcely any improvement in lo-
comotion or comfort except at the expense of noise.
If we introduce a new material (like iron) into the
construction of our houses or ships, we find that we
have simply added a new anguish to the ordinary experience of life. In sensitive natures the whole brain
becomes, under the everlasting trip-hammer of this
infernal pandemonium of noise, like a huge sore exposed to the blows of a lash, and there are men and
women in numbers greater than we shall ever guess,
who have gone mad under this fiendish pounding and
jarring and screaming of the world's noise.

There has been motive enough, therefore, for the
abatement of this curse, if any body were competent
to abate it. There are some of us who would give a
good deal more than we pay for most luxuries if we
could hush these feverish streets and avenues into
stillness, and if, without arresting all the eager life
of a great city, we could so order it that that life
should go on, and that its warehouses and dwellings
should go up, without the blows of the workmen, the
sharp scream of the saw, the fierce thunder of the iron
joist, or the endless rattle and clatter of uncounted
noise-breeders and noise-transmitters, besides. But
somehow, it can not be. No modern structure was
ever lifted to its place in such majestic silence as that
which attended upon the building of Solomon's Temple; nor is it likely that such a thing soon will be.

And thus the rearing of the temple becomes, not so much an example for literal imitation, as it is a prophecy of ultimate realization. That peculiar and exceptional method of building which was adopted in the case of the temple must have had a reason for it, and that reason must have been a divine reason. It did not occur to this semibarbarous people to build the temple in this way. The method was revealed to them. What was its reason? Doubtless, in the first place, to educate a race with imperfect ideas of reverence into a higher conception of the sacredness of divine things. The average Jew entered the temple with a deeper awe when he remembered the august sanctities with which its erection had been hedged about. We do the same thing to-day, when, in building a church, we put up a notice that all boisterous or profane language is to be avoided on the part of the workmen. But there must have been something more in such a command as that referred to in the text, and there was. Says the apostle, speaking of the pathetic story of Hagar and Ishmael, and their expulsion by Abram at the jealous bidding of Sarah, "Which things are an allegory." Just so, here was an allegory. This childish people needed to be taught, in many ways and with most laborious painstaking the great lesson of the higher meaning of life. And so, the building of the temple was itself, made at once a stately and solemn prophecy of that, for which men are put here in this world, and then of the relations of this present world and life, to a life and world to come. The thing that must instantly occur to us, the moment that we have read about the silent way in which this temple-building was prepared for and accomplished, is that, after all the noise was not gotten rid of; but simply separated from the ultimate construction. You can not quarry a stone without noise. No huge boulder was ever lifted out of its primeval bed or riven from its parent rock without blows and sweat and strain and thunderous percussion. No tree was ever felled without that sharp smiting and steady thud of the workman's axe which has made ten thousand forests ring. In handling the metals which we employ in rearing any lowliest temple, with what a heat and noise those metals must be forged! Nay, if we could have been among the craftsmen at Mount Lebanon where the timbers of the temple where prepared and the stones for its foundations hewn and dressed, we should have found there no lack of clamor, and strife and unrest. No least detail of that holy and beautiful house was made ready save at the cost of countless blows, of manifold discussion, of ceaseless weariness and fatigue. Doubtless there were there all the catastrophes, the maladjustments, the sacrifice of individual life or limb to a great undertaking that there are in similar undertakings to-day. The reason why "there was neither hammer nor axe nor any tool of iron heard in the house while it was in building" was because for days and weeks and months beforehand there had been incessant noise, untiring toil, infinite and undiscouraged pounding and smoothing and planing and hammering, almost night and day. And do you suppose there was nothing more? The men who built the temple were not angels, but children of a race trained by long bondage to the chain and the lash. Pharaoh's task-masters had beaten them when the tale of bricks was short. Is it likely that Solomon's task-masters were persons of such pre-eminent gentleness and infinite patience that they never struck a blow or spoke a harsh word? If we could have the unwritten history of that splendid building I presume we should find that its stones were moistened more than once with the salt tears of workmen who had not always done their best, or who, striving to do it, had not always and instantly achieved the best result. This huge task was not accomplished without cost, and here, as always in the achievement of any great work the costliest expenditure was not in money, but in human sweat and in human sorrow.

But the time came when the strain and the sorrow were ended. The time came when every least detail had been wrought out with uttermost and absolute excellence, and was ready to be lifted to its place. And then with what a glad surprise they themselves who had hewn some stone or carved some capital or smoothed some stately cedar saw these disjointed fragments lifted finally to their places. The era of noise was ended. No sharp cry, no grinding tool, no jarring blow broke the sublime stillness. Swiftly but surely, as though by some magic power, the majestic temple rose. A man who had toiled upon some segment of its portals or corridors, wondering in his dull way how such a shape could be of service, saw with a thrill of delight, the great arches reach out from side to side, like the mercy and truth of the Psalmist, to kiss each other, and lo ! his task had been to carve the keystone. A workman in the precious metals, forging a copper plate in form and ornamentation equally unintelligible, beheld his burnished handiwork take at last its place, flashing thence upon his vision like some star in a heavenly constellation. How noble and how beautiful every least detail, but above all, how wonderful this absolute adaptedness of every related part to the grand and majestic whole !

And it was thus, that, as to-day, we teach children by cards and pictures and models, God began long ago, to teach His earlier children, by this great picture and model, the meaning of human life. How we hate noise, some of us, and long that our life may be free from it ! As society grows more refined and conventional we proscribe all needless noise by laws of utmost rigor. If the servant slams the door, he must find a place where people do not care to have doors shut noiselessly. We do. If any one has a loud voice or laugh, or moves about in a way that creates jar and clatter, he must be taught, as swiftly and sternly as possible, that these offences are rather more grave than breaking the ten commandments. The best adjustment of the social machinery demands not decorum merely, but noiselessness.

But we are not very successful, after all, in getting it. Life refuses to be so adjusted as to eliminate from it all strife and conflict and pain. There are a thousand tasks that, in larger interests than ours, must be done, whether we want them or no. The world refuses to walk upon tip-toe so that we may be able to sleep. It gets up very early and stays up very late, and all the while there is the conflict of ten million hammers and saws and axes with the stubborn material that in no other way can be made to serve its use and do its work for man. And then too, these hammers and axes are not wielded without train or pang, but wring from the millions of toilers who labor with them, cries and groans and tears. Nay, our own toil, our temple-building, whether it be for God or man, exacts its bitter toll and fills life with cries and blows. The thousand rivalries of our daily business, the fierce animosities when we are beaten, the even fiercer exultation when we have beaten, the crashing blows of disaster, the piercing scream of defeat,—these things we have not yet gotten rid of, nor in this life ever will.

Why should we wish to get rid of them? You are here my brother, to be hewn and planed and hammered in God's quarry and on God's anvil for a nobler life to come. We are wont when we look at life in its highest aspect to dwell chiefly upon its individual needs and its personal destiny. And this is right. There is no question in all the world so important to you, to me, as the question—What is your personal relation—what is mine—to the Being who has made us and redeemed us? But even in answering that question we can not leave out of sight the fact that our life is not merely individual but also related. We are solitary souls. Yes. But then we are associated souls. The family means that. The Church means that. Society and the state mean that. And the family here means a family there. The Church and the state and society here, mean a higher and diviner society yet to be, of which these earthly fellowships are at once the training school and the vestibule. But is any one of us here ready for that upper fellowship, meet for that heavenly temple, as he is? What is it that makes the discipline of life so necessary even for those of us who have no conception or aspiration beyond the present? We would gladly house our children from the rough usage of the world and hedge them about by the gentler handling of their homes. But we say, nevertheless, that it is well for a boy to go out into the world—to face the contradictions and collisions of life—to have, as we phrase it, the "rough corners knocked off from him," and we are right. But the boy's need is ours as well. There is many a tall cedar of Lebanon the rank luxuriance of whose growth means only ultimate rot and ruin. A man, like a tree, if he is to serve his noblest use, needs to be hewn and seasoned. The axe must be laid at the root of many a stately oak, not that it may die, but that it may live. The sharp discipline of pain, the keen blade that lops away the superfluous branches, the crashing fall that lays us low now, so that finally we may be lifted up on high,—these are the things which can not be left out of any life, any more than blows and axes and hammers can be spared from any earthly building. What is more horrible than war? and yet the most memorable wars have simply been God driving a nail on which to hang some eternal principle of truth and righteousness, or quarrying foundations on which have arisen the enduring greatness of whole peoples.

Now, then, bring all this home to your own personal experience. Most of us, when we think of life, have a double grievance: first of all that it is so turbulent and unquiet, so never-ceasing in its clash of tools and whirl of thunderous machinery. But can you make any thing without the ring of the hammer or the scream of the saw? Can you drive an engine without the pounding and hammering of the million rivets that hold together its boiler? When you go into a quarry or forge, do you expect the silence of a desert or the hush of a drawing-room? No! You know that all this noise means ultimate and worthy construction, and that the building, whether of a temple or of a civilization, is impossible without it.

Do not expect silence, then, any more in the moral and spiritual world. God is at work there, quarrying the rock which in its turn, resting upon the Rock of Ages, shall make the temple of the future. These wars and famines, these pangs and outcries are His heavenly hewing and shaping whereby, sooner or later, that city and that temple shall be builded whose builder and maker is God!

And so, too, of that other grievance which is more selfish and personal. "If there must be all this unrest and clamor and cost," we say, " so be it, but why need it wound and bruise me? Why must I have my will crossed and my affections lacerated and my pride humbled by these blows which seem sometimes to fall, so cruelly thick and fast?" Only, my brother, because the life that you are living here is not, as you are tempted to account it, an end, but simply a means to an end. You are calculating how you can acquire a fortune, or win a reputation, or climb into a lofty and enviable station. You think that if you had

only this or that gift which another has, life for you
would be ripe and round and perfect. And then, instead of winning it, there comes broken health, or
domestic bitterness, or a lonely lot, or business failure and ruin. You are soured and embittered as you
think how different your life might have been, if only
yours had been the lot of that other, the favorite of
fortune, whose perfumed splendors taunt you as you
meet them. Your life!—which life? the life outermost
or the life innermost? the life of your tastes or the life
of your soul, the life that is, or the life that is to
come? Ah! I think that some of us will wonder
when we stand upon the farther shore and drink of
the blessedness of that life, how we could have re-
pined at the hardness and bitterness of this! As that
prisoner whom the French Revolution liberated from
the Bastile and who hung up his fetters in his English
home that looking on them he might bless the bitter
discipline that had taught him the sweetness of liberty, even so we, looking down and back on the quar-
ries where we were hewn and sculptured, will thank
God for every wound, and bless Him for the sharp
tools and stern blows that cut loose from us those
coarse and selfish encrustations of the life of sense.

And this brings me to a question at once practical
and personal. This Sunday falls in the Season of
Lent. A wisdom wiser than ours has bidden us to
try for a little while the effect of a voluntary absti-

nence and self-discipline. I have no special rules to offer you—no Procrustean bed upon which to stretch alike all our various natures. But you know your own nature. You know well enough, or if you do not you very easily may, whether any lust of the flesh, or of the mind, any inordinate desire is eating into your spiritual life and so rotting it to death. Are you the master of your own appetites, you own slothful, self-indulgent, petulant, envious slanderous dispositions, or are they your masters?

What is the good of Lent? do you ask. Well, if it is good for nothing else, Lent is good for that. No matter who invented it, or how it came, here are forty days in which the Church of God asks you to examine yourself and find out what kind of a life you are living and whither it is tending. If you are perfectly clear on this point,—if you have no tempers nor appetites to be chastened, no faith to be quickened, no sin to be repented of, no coldness to lament, then, verily Lent has no message for you and you have no use for Lent. But if it is otherwise, then some time or other must be a good time for doing these things, and if, in spite of all the sneers and ridicule which one hears, a good many people are striving to do them at this time, then it is at least worth while to consider whether this time may not be a good time for you to do them.

You have a higher destiny than as yet perhaps you

have recognized. God forbid that you should miss it because you will not own His call! He calls you to be a stone in His living and eternal temple. Do your part to make yourself meet for so high and holy a calling! Chasten your selfishness. Discipline and master your coarser hungers. Curb and humble your pride and your impatience. Do these things as He shall help you to do them and as the cross of His dear Son shall quicken and inspire you. And then, when sorrow comes, when the blow falls, when the knife cuts, when the old tendrils are rent and bleeding, and your soul cries out from under His bitter chastening,—then, blessed be His holy name, that soul can still sing its trust:

> "He comes and lays my heart, all heated,
>   On the hard anvil, minded so
> Into His own fair shape to beat it
>   With His great hammer, blow on blow;
> And yet I whisper—as God will!
> And at His heaviest blows hold still.

>   .   .   .   .

> "He kindles for my profit surely
>   Affliction's glowing, fiery brand,
> And all His heaviest blows are surely
>   Inflicted by a Master hand:
> So I say, praying—as God will!
> And hope in Him, and suffer still." *

---

* Julius Sturm, in "Hymns of the Ages," second series.